stasi eldredge

beautiful now

*90 days of experiencing
God's dreams for you*

David C Cook

transforming lives together

BEAUTIFUL NOW
Published by David C Cook
4050 Lee Vance View
Colorado Springs, CO 80918 U.S.A.

David C Cook Distribution Canada
55 Woodslee Avenue, Paris, Ontario, Canada N3L 3E5

David C Cook U.K., Kingsway Communications
Eastbourne, East Sussex BN23 6NT, England

The graphic circle C logo is a registered trademark of David C Cook.

LCCN 2015944623
ISBN 978-0-7814-1407-4
eISBN 978-0-7814-1431-9

© 2016 Stasi Eldredge
Published in association with Yates & Yates, www.yates2.com

The Team: Alice Crider, Elisa Stanford, Amy Konyndyk,
Helen Macdonald, Susan Murdock
Cover Design: Nick Lee

Printed in the United States of America
First Edition 2016

1 2 3 4 5 6 7 8 9 10

101515

To Susie, Em, and Olivia:
You are beautiful gifts to
my heart and life.

contents

introduction *9*

1   the unveiling *11*

2   what God has promised *13*

3   the secret *15*

4   let hope rise *17*

5   an inside-out process *19*

6   glorious mess *21*

7   God knows *23*

8   God dreams big *25*

9   what can God not do? *27*

10   come and drink *29*

11   great expectations *31*

12   creating space *33*

13   desperate for God *35*

14   divine interruptions *37*

15   the broken road *39*

16   rewriting your story *41*

17   created in the image of God *43*

18   more than conquerors *46*

19   coheirs with Christ *49*

20   beautiful girl *51*

21   healing memories *53*

22	invite Jesus here	. . . .	55
23	God's lullaby	. . . .	58
24	the only reflection that matters	. . .	60
25	Jesus is the goal	. . . .	62
26	God loves quirky	. . . .	64
27	embracing God's good work	. . . .	66
28	a higher truth	. . . .	68
29	risk dreaming	. . . .	70
30	wanting what God wants	. . . . .	72
31	a tender heart	. . . .	74
32	living life on purpose	. . . . . .	76
33	inhabiting your beauty	. . . . . .	78
34	a shining light	. . . .	80
35	a quality of spirit	. . . .	82
36	live boldly	. . . .	84
37	what will God say?	. . . . . .	87
38	losing ourselves	. . . .	89
39	out of control	. . . .	91
40	God's greatest command	. . . .	93
41	can we trust God?	. . . . . .	95
42	the only safe place	. . . . . .	98
43	*all* your needs	. . . .	100
44	fearless	. . . .	102
45	one of his own	. . . .	104
46	just believe	. . . .	106

47	the final word	108
48	a heavenly exchange	110
49	saying yes to God's plan	112
50	the power of friendships	114
51	forever friends	116
52	satisfaction	118
53	perfect love	120
54	surrendering	122
55	our biggest cheerleaders	124
56	jealousy and envy	126
57	bff?	128
58	honestly	131
59	let it go	134
60	crucified to the world	136
61	treasures	138
62	the window of grace	141
63	floodwaters	143
64	true victory	145
65	far from eden	147
66	the doorway of suffering	150
67	acquainted with grief	152
68	beauty from ashes	154
69	finding peace	156
70	leaning into God	158
71	the work of suffering	160

72	giving thanks	162
73	beautiful scars	164
74	shake off your dust	166
75	where freedom begins	169
76	no longer captives	172
77	free to fail	174
78	the fight of faith	176
79	agreeing with God	178
80	worthy of our yes	180
81	an active imagination	182
82	when God lingers	184
83	lavish love	186
84	you are chosen	189
85	a divine exchange	191
86	"she was with Jesus"	194
87	your true name	197
88	what the world needs now	199
89	who do you think you are?	201
90	you are the beloved	204

a few final words from stasi 206

introduction

Did you know you are beautiful? Right at this moment? Regardless of your body shape, your teeth whiteness, your skin tone, or the wrongs you've done in your life—maybe the wrongs you've done just this morning.

When God looks at you, he does not view you through the veil of your sin, the shroud of your failures, or the canopy of your past. When God looks at you, he sees you through the blood of Jesus. When God looks at you, he sees the righteousness of Jesus Christ. You are a spotless, pure, stunning bride. Oh, how we need to see ourselves as he does!

Though we don't always acknowledge our own beauty and we often dream of becoming beautiful, God sees us as *beautiful now*. It's not a "someday" thing for him. He sees *you* as beautiful—today and every day—and he wants you to see what he sees.

If you read my book *Becoming Myself*, hopefully you began to embrace God's dream *of* you. Join me now in *experiencing* God's dream *for* you—the dream in which you and your life are beautiful now. Each day in this three-month devotional includes a Scripture verse or passage, a word of encouragement from me, and then a prayer, question, or a declaration for you to use as a starting point for your own intimate time with God.

Come, my sister, let's press on to the goal set before us—to be fully transformed, fully alive, fully ourselves, fully his. You are in the palm of his hand, and nothing can take you out. As you lean on Jesus more and more, calling on him to live through your life, you are transformed into the image of God. You discover the brilliant truth that the more of his you become, the more yourself you become.

There are no qualifications in God's eyes of love. He does not look at you and say, "You're beautiful *when … if … but …*" He looks at you and says, "You are beautiful. Now."

1

---

the unveiling

*So all of us who have had that veil removed can see
and reflect the glory of the Lord. And the Lord—who
is the Spirit—makes us more and more like him
as we are changed into his glorious image.*
—2 Corinthians 3:18 NLT

God is in the business of setting us free. Making us
into the women he always wanted us to be. The women
we always wanted to be. Sometimes he makes changes
with the flip of a switch. But not most of the time (as
you well know). Most of the time God invites us into
a *process* of change—a process through which by grace
we can rise to the occasion of our lives.

It is a beautiful paradox that the more of *God's* we
become, the more *ourselves* we become—the self he had
in mind when he thought of you before the creation of
the world. She's in there; she might be badly bruised

and covered with all sorts of muck, but she's in there. And Jesus comes to call her out.

God is *unveiling* who we truly are. All those veils of shame and sin and the false self, all those veils others have put upon us, thinking they know who we ought to be—God takes them all away so that with unveiled faces we might reflect his glory.

The process often feels slow, interminable even. But lasting change takes time. Anyone can muscle through a day; New Year's resolutions may even last a few months. But God is a God of process, and he has his eye on eternity. His plans for us aren't for a quick fix but an eternal transformation. Slowly. Carefully. Intentionally. The unveiling is taking place.

Jesus, give me a glimpse of who you are calling me to be today. Help me see the unveiling happening in my life even now. I want to see myself as you see me.

2

---

what God has promised

For God knew his people in advance, and he chose
them to become like his Son, so that his Son would
be the firstborn among many brothers and sisters.
—Romans 8:29 NLT

Does anybody ever really change? I believe they do. I've
seen it happen. The Scriptures promise it can happen. It's
happening in me. God has come for me, and he continues
to come for me. He has healed me, and he continues to
heal me. He has saved me, and he is saving me still,
crafting his beauty and presence more deeply into my
soul. "I Am" has taken up residence, and his very presence is changing me. He who is utterly himself is
enabling me to become myself, the self he had in mind
when he made me.

Sure, I still tend to replay conversations I've had
with others in my head, looking for my mistakes, but I
linger in self-contempt less these days. Yes, I still reach

for carbohydrates when the only thing hungry is my soul, but I do it less often. I am growing in knowing that I am completely loved in this moment and that God isn't waiting for me to get my act together in order to become worthy of his affection. I have only and ever been lovely to God, and so have you. In the steady face of his love, I am changing. I am becoming myself.

I know you have tried to change and hoped for change in the past. Today God is inviting you to hope again. By *faith*. We cannot heal ourselves or free ourselves or save ourselves. We cannot become ourselves all by ourselves. But we are not by ourselves. We are seen and known and strengthened and urged on to the life we were created for by the King of Love. He wants to help us to become. He wants to help us change and grow. We can't do it, but *he can*. He's very, very good at it. It is, in fact, what he has promised to do.

I choose to believe today that God's presence in me is changing me! I can't change myself, but he can and will help me change and grow.

3

the secret

This is the secret: Christ lives in you. This
gives you assurance of sharing his glory.
—Colossians 1:27 NLT

The paradox of change is that it involves surrendering ourselves to God, giving everything over to him—including all our efforts to change and all our resignation that we'll never change.

Then God restores us—the real us. Once we surrender ourselves, he gives us back our true selves. In fact, the most important journey any woman will take is the journey into becoming herself through the love of God. It is a journey that will require courage, faith, and above all a willingness to grow and to let go. The journey of becoming is one of increased self-awareness coupled with a surrender of self. It is a dance between choosing and yielding, desiring and relinquishing, trying and giving up.

Is there a way to hasten the change we long for in our lives? Yes. Accelerating our "becoming" involves saying yes to God again and again and again. It is not a posture of striving but of releasing. It looks a lot more like yielding than pushing through to the next goal. We collapse into God's life within us. "Christ in me, help me" becomes our prayer. That is why he often brings us to the end of our ropes, the end of ourselves. Because it is from there we turn from our striving and raise our arms in surrender to our God *again* to save us.

By faith we turn to him. By faith we choose to believe that he hears our prayer. By faith we believe he is good and is for us. By faith we trust that though we may not see it or feel it, God is at work in us and for us. Because he says he is.

Jesus, I say yes to you. I say yes to who you say I am. I say yes to the beauty you see in me. I say yes to your power to change me. I say yes to you in me, at work in me, and for me.

4

---

let hope rise

*The steadfast love of the L*ORD *never ceases; his mercies never come to an end; they are new every morning; great is your faithfulness.*
—Lamentations 3:22–23 ESV

Sometimes we feel hopeless to ever change simply because our personal history is filled with our failed attempts to change. Where was that angel who was supposed to be guarding our tongue and preventing those harsh words from lashing out at our children? What happened to that fruit of the Spirit that was empowering us to be self-controlled and pass by the donut section? God has not given me a spirit of fear, so why am I so consumed with worry over my children, my finances, my future? If the fear of man is a snare, why do I still find I am terrified of exposing my true self and then being rejected? My bondage to food has been revealed as a liar and a thief, and yet in the moment of pain, too often I still turn to it.

God knows. He has not turned his face away. The very fact that we long for the change we do is a sign that *we are meant to have it*. Our very dissatisfaction with our weaknesses and struggles points to the reality that continuing to live in them is not our destiny.

Why are you struggling with the things you do? There is a reason. It is found in the life you have lived, the wounds you have received, what you have come to believe about yourself because of them, and not having a clue how to bear your sorrow. It is also because of who you are meant to be.

It is not too late. It is not too hard. You are not too much. God's mercies are new every morning. There is mercy in his eyes even now.

What changes do you long for in your life today? What does your desire say about the woman God created you to be?

5
———

an inside-out process

Apart from me you can do nothing.
—John 15:5 ESV

In this process of becoming who God created us to be, we need to remember that shame and discipline are not agents of lasting change.

Like a shot of caffeine in the morning, self-loathing may propel us onto the road of change, but we will find that hatred of self only leads us onto a never-ending roundabout.

Self-discipline isn't going to cut it either. Discipline, particularly spiritual discipline, is a holy and good thing, one that increases over a lifetime of practice. But when we lean on it alone to bring about the change we long for, we find that the fruit is *not* a grace-filled woman. We get angry. We get discouraged. Trying, striving, working harder may get us through the week, but it won't take us through the decades.

True transformation cannot be forced from the outside. It's an inside-out process. Who of us has not received or created a list of ways to live, eat, exercise, respond, seek God, grow, and change—and how long did it last, if it worked at all? Those lists don't work very long for *anyone*, and so we fall back into self-contempt. The problem does not lie with our lack of discipline. The problem is in the approach.

When we have a change of heart on the inside, it manifests itself on the outside, not the other way around. God invites us to join him in the process through which he heals our inner world so he can transform our outer world.

The voice of shame says, *I hate me; I need to get rid of me.* The voice of discipline says, *I've got to fix me because me is not good.* God says, *I love you; let me restore you.* I like that one best.

In what ways do you rely on shame or self-discipline to try to change yourself, rather than relying on God's work in you?

---

glorious mess

The Word became flesh and blood,
and moved into the neighborhood.
—John 1:14 MSG

Our transformation begins when we believe we are loved. Born out of love, into love, to know love, and to be loved. Yes, we were born into a fallen, sorry world, which is at the same time more lovely than any fairy tale. And in this beautiful, heartbreaking world, God—the eternal, omniscient, amazing One—loves human beings. Including you. Especially you.

You were born into a glorious mess, and we all have become something of a glorious mess ourselves. And in the midst of our mess, God has a thing for us. He does not despise our humanity or despair over our condition as we sometimes do. He does not turn his face away from us in our failings or our self-centeredness, as we would like to. He is not *surprised*. He is aware that we are but dust and he has made arrangements for us to not stay that way.

Let me say this truth again: you are loved. Deeply. Profoundly. Unimaginably loved. And you are a wondrous creature. Whether you are having victory in every area of your life or not. Whether you just lost your temper (again) or indulged in a fantasy, another cookie, or thoughts of self-contempt. You are loved. Right here in this very moment, you are loved and pursued and seen by the One who sees everything. He knows you better than you know yourself, and you have never been a disappointment to him.

Dear Jesus, though this is difficult for me to experience sometimes, I choose to believe the beautiful truth that you love me no matter what. I surrender to you again, right now. I am yours! I pray this in the name of Jesus Christ! Amen.

God knows

For the Son of Man came to seek and to save the lost.
—Luke 19:10

Food addiction has always been a struggle for me. But God is not going to love me any more or any differently when and if I finally lose weight and become free from the stranglehold of food. Jesus's love for me, my Father's love for me, never changes. My fellowship with God may be strained at times, but his heart toward me does not change. He is passionately in love with me. Even better, I think he likes me.

And by the way, he's got a pretty huge thing for you too. Yes, you. Becoming who God created you to be does not change God's love for you. The truth is, he could not love you any more than he does in this moment. You are not disappointing him now. You may be disappointed, but he is not. Jesus knew what he was in for when he came "to seek and to save the lost." He came to seek and to save *all* that was lost—in our loving and living and dreaming and longing. He has saved us, and he is saving us still. We are being transformed into the very image of Christ. Whether we feel like it or not.

I know that most days, we don't feel as if we're being transformed into God's image with "ever-increasing glory" (2 Cor. 3:18). It's a mess. But God is in the mess. He is about transforming our inner mess so he can transform the rest of the mess. Jesus understands our struggles and our sorrows. He knows our hearts have been broken, and he has come to heal them. He knows we long to change. He knows what needs to happen and where. He knows what is in the way. Though we are too much for ourselves, we are not too much for him.

I choose to believe today that I am loved, wanted, seen, delighted in, provided for, cherished, chosen, known, and planned. I am set apart, believed in, invited, valued, and blessed!

8

God dreams big

For as the sky soars high above earth,
so the way I work surpasses the way you work,
and the way I think is beyond the way you think.
—Isaiah 55:9 MSG

So, who are you? A great way to discover the answer to that is simply to ask, what do you like? What would you do with your life if you were free to do anything at all?

A number of years ago in a small group, my husband, John, shared some thoughts about desire, that core place in our hearts where God speaks. Then he invited each of us to write down what we wanted. To write a long list. Not to edit it. Nothing was too small or too large to write down. My list turned out to be two pages long and had things on it as varied as the garden I wanted to nurture, the hope to ride horses with my husband, the healing I longed for a few dear ones to experience, and the wedding of a single friend I wanted to dance at.

I found that list a few years ago, and to my astonishment every single item had come true. It had happened!

God dreams big. And he invites us to dream big with him. He has planted dreams and desires in each one of our hearts that are unique to us. Opening up our spirits, our minds, our hearts, our imaginations to what we would really like—to even the possibility of wanting—allows the Holy Spirit to awaken parts of ourselves that are in such a deep sleep that no dreams are happening.

God is a dreamer. He has dreams of you and for you. What dreams might he have for you today?

If you had unlimited resources, what would you do with your time and money in the next year?

9

---

what can God not do?

"For I know the plans I have for you," declares
the LORD, "plans to prosper you and not to harm
you, plans to give you hope and a future."
—Jeremiah 29:11

When we dream with God, we don't want to start thinking immediately, *How can I make this happen?* Dreaming with God isn't about *how*. It's about *what*. If anything could happen, then what would I love to see happen in my life? What would I love to see happen in the lives of those I love?

It's much easier to dream for other people, to have desires for our children and our friends. We can fairly easily name what we want their lives to look like, the healing and the freedom we'd love for them to come to know. It's a wee bit more difficult to dream for our own lives.

But this book is about *your* heart. This moment is about your dreams and your desires that contribute to the unique, marvelous woman you are. The point is not so much being able to name the desire as it is to allow God to access the places in our hearts where dreams and desires are planted. God speaks to us there. About himself. About ourselves.

It's okay to want, and it's okay to want *more*. Wanting more has nothing to do with feeling unsatisfied or lacking in your present reality. It's being open to the more that God wants to bring to you in your life. The possibilities for you are limitless! Yes, they are. Maybe not for tomorrow but for your *life*.

What can God not do? What is too hard for him to accomplish in your relationships, achievements, creativity, and in the fullness of the expression of who you are? We want to be women who continue to grow all our lives. We never want to stop. Yes, we rest. But a heart alive is a heart that is awake and curious and pressing in to more.

Lord, help me dream the dreams you have of me and for me. Today I let go of how they can happen, and I open my heart and mind to all the possibilities you have for me. In Jesus's name, amen.

10

come and drink

Let anyone who is thirsty come to me and drink.
—John 7:37

We are spiritually thirsty women, and that is a very good thing. It may not be *comfortable*, but it is good. If you aren't aware of your hunger, you're not very motivated to go to the banquet table. If you aren't aware of your thirst, you don't seek something to drink. Studies show that when a person finally becomes aware of their physical thirst, they are already dehydrated. We are all thirstier than we realize.

In our world we are barraged with options as to how to quench our thirst. We are buried in advertisements and information and suggestions and ideas and products and programs and *have you heard the latest?* Catalogs and flyers are felling forests to offer an answer to our ache, to assuage our thirst.

I have tried a lot of them. I've bought the shoes, read the book, done the study, and attended the program. I'm still thirsty. Scientists warn that the ability to be aware of and respond to thirst is slowly blunted as we age. In a world that oftentimes feels as dry as a desert, we can become numb to our own thirst.

As women who are being transformed into the image of Christ, we don't want to grow numb. We want to grow increasingly thirsty. I've tried to assuage my thirsty heart with the mirror, with accomplishments, with relationships. I still need something to drink. I need the Living Water himself. So do you. This is our most precious fundamental need. We have heard the alluring sound of flowing, life-giving water, and we have come to the river.

Jesus, I am thirsty for you today. I know that nothing else will satisfy my thirst. Help me see how I am seeking to quench my thirst in other ways, so that I can turn back to you. Amen.

11

---

great expectations

For with God nothing will be impossible.
—Luke 1:37 RSV

Our life of faith is uncertain, but we can expect good. Because we belong to God, we can rest in knowing that his promises to us are true and he is faithful. It's not a question of if God is going to show up but how and when. It is not a question of *if* he is going to move on our behalf but of *how* he will. It isn't even a question of if he is going to continue pursuing and wooing us deeper into his heart filled with affection for us but of if we will recognize him. We can live with joyful expectancy! There are no ifs with God. The only ifs relate to us.

If we will trust him.

If we will believe him.

If we will ask him.

If we will continue to ask him.

How God loves his people to ask him in faith—pressing in, continuing to ask no matter how long it takes, believing that he will come through for us.

I recently spoke with a friend who has been praying for her children to come to know Jesus for thirty years. Sometimes she loses hope and needs others to carry her hope for a while. But she continues to pray and believe. She's right to do so. Because, really, what's too difficult for God? A virgin giving birth? God himself becoming a man and living among us? God coming for *you*? Coming to you in your thirst and in your uncertainty?

As the angel Gabriel told Mary, *nothing* is too difficult for our God.

God, help me to keep turning to you, to keep trusting, to keep believing that nothing is impossible for you.

12

creating space

He brought me out into a spacious place;
he rescued me because he delighted in me.
—Psalm 18:19

We have to have space in our lives in order to have room for wonder, joy, and awe—in order to have room for God! We all have choices we must make to protect that space for him to come. We can't do everything or please everyone. Sometimes we have to say, "I'm sorry, but I can't make that." Or, "I'm sorry—and this is not a reflection of you or of my desire to help—but my life is too full right now." Or simply, "No."

I know that when we say no, we risk offending people. We risk disappointing them. But if we don't say no—if we refuse empty spaces and only fill our lives with busyness and people pleasing—then we risk losing something much more important. We sacrifice the quality of ourselves that makes us women of worth, substance, and depth. We fill all the space ourselves and leave God out. A full life does not equal a beautiful one. A busy life does not equal a joyful one.

Choose space. Choose margin. Choose Jesus. He loves to come and fill voids with light and life, but first you must have a void for him to fill. We do not need to fear the emptiness. Not in our schedules, not in our lives, and not in our hearts. We simply need to invite Jesus into the empty and sacred spaces—and guard our open, waiting hearts as the treasures that they are.

Dearest Jesus, I choose you first and foremost. I give you the hours of my day, and I ask for your help not to fill them with unnecessary busyness but to leave space to encounter your love and beauty. I'm uncomfortable with stillness, God, but you are not. I ask you as well to give me the courage I need to say no to the people and projects that you would have me say no to! I trust you with my life and with my relationships. So, help me now, Lord, to quiet myself, and I invite you to come and meet with me. I need you. In Jesus's name.

13

desperate for God

As a deer pants for flowing streams,
so pants my soul for you, O God.
—Psalm 42:1 ESV

Each one of us has a place in our life where we are not living in the victory we long for. Our struggle might be rooted in our past, in a fear of intimacy, or in a need to control our world. That broken place changes how we view ourselves—and makes us desperate for God.

We all have something that brings us to our knees. It isn't something we would ever choose for ourselves or wish on anyone else, but we all have an area—or ten!— in our lives that drives us to need God. We can't free ourselves. We are weak, aware that something inside is broken and starving. It is a wonderful grace when we finally give up and fall down before the One who is strong.

And, my friend, it is not a bad thing that you desperately need Jesus. For some reason we feel embarrassed by our desperation; we see desperation as a sign that something is terribly wrong with us. Oh, no. We were created to desperately need Jesus. We have always needed him, and we always will. I do not believe God caused the pain of our lives, but I do know he uses it to drive us to him.

Father, I believe you work all things together for my good, even the hard things. I ask you to use the areas that I am struggling in today to draw my heart closer to yours. I need you more than I need victory in every area. Reveal your love to me today, Father, here in my weakness. You be my strength. I look to you. In Jesus's name.

14

---

divine interruptions

Before they call I will answer;
while they are still speaking I will hear.
—Isaiah 65:24

Do you ever catch yourself thinking, *I have to prove myself as worthy to God if he's going to do anything good in my life?* Or maybe you think, *Miracles may happen to other people, but I'm not good enough for them to happen to me!*

The miraculous is not a strange thing to God. *The miraculous is his normal.* Divinely interrupting our lives is not an extraordinary event. Supernaturally showing up, speaking into the heart, and creating a longing for himself—this is his realm. He speaks to us. He leads us. He heals us. He presses into us with his manifest presence as we reach out to him. He moves through us with power, revealing his glory. God has come. God will come. God loves to come.

Not only that, but God likes rescuing his people! He likes rescuing *you*. He enjoys coming through in dramatic ways. Scripture is rife with stories of God stacking the deck against his ability to rescue or save, and then—*pow!*—he proves himself amazing and involved once again. He wants to do the same thing in your life today. Pray for him to come into your heart in a new, miraculous way right now. Then expect that he will.

God, thank you for being ready and eager to perform miracles in my heart and my life. I expect and accept them!

15

the broken road

To him who is able to keep you from stumbling and to present you before his glorious presence without fault and with great joy—to the only God our Savior be glory, majesty, power and authority, through Jesus Christ our Lord, before all ages, now and forevermore! Amen.
—Jude 24–25

So often I wish I could go back in time and change my words or actions. *If only I knew then what I know now! If only I had just kept my mouth shut! Why did I do that, say that, want that?* Still, I realize the reason I am where I am is because of the journey I have been on. And not just the lovely "I'd love to do that again" parts of my journey either. The ugly parts too. I got here from there.

I would love to change much of my story, particularly the times when my struggles and failures have caused my family and friends grief. But God is in their stories as well. And so with an open hand, surrounded by grace, I learn and begin again. I remember and step forward.

It may seem strange that at certain points on our journey we need to look back in order to continue moving forward, but it's true. Forgetting our mistakes, victories, challenges, sorrows—our *story*—prevents us from moving forward and growing into the women God created us to be. Remembering is a part of becoming.

The temptation is to look back with regret rather than with mercy. But God's eyes see clearly, and they are filled with mercy.

Though our past has shaped us, we are not our past. Though our failures and sin have had an effect on who we are, they do not define us. Though thought patterns and addictions have overwhelmed us, we are not overcome by them and we will never be overcome by them. Jesus has won our victory. Jesus is our victory.

I take hold today of the victory that Jesus won for me on the cross. I choose to move forward from my mistakes, receiving God's mercy. I know that my weaknesses do not define me; Jesus's work on the cross defines me.

16

---

rewriting your story

Have mercy on me, my God, have mercy on me,
for in you I take refuge....
Awake, my soul!
—Psalm 57:1, 8

No matter your past, God can rewrite your story. Your story is *his* story, really, and one day he will tell it in all of its hidden splendor. You will get to find out what was going on behind the scenes. He will share with you the ways he was working all things together for your good. It will be marvelous to hear. Because God has been loving you, shielding you, and delighting in you—though now you do not see it as clearly as you will one day.

Invite God to show you your past through his eyes. Ask him to surface good memories you have forgotten. He would love to do it. He wants to lead you to healing. He wants to replace regret with mercy.

, The stories from your past that shaped you and the words spoken over your life that have crippled you do not stand a chance in the light of the powerful grace and mercy that come to us now in the Person of Jesus. You do not have to remain captive any longer. The holy work of God deep in your heart as you have suffered is stunning beyond measure. You may not see the goodness yet, but you will. You will one day see your life through God's loving eyes.

Jesus is inviting you to recover those parts of yourself you have tried to hide in the hopes of being more acceptable to him. He knows the parts of your personality you want to change, the dreams you've buried, the wounds you have ignored. The Holy Spirit wants to kiss you awake. So come, my beloved. Awaken. Remember. Jesus has come to heal us and restore us to himself, to others, and even to ourselves.

Dear God, help me see my past through your eyes. Help me see how you use even the very painful parts of my story to bring good, to do a holy work in me.

17

---

created in the image of God

So God created man in his own image,
in the image of God he created him;
male and female he created them.
—Genesis 1:27 ESV

Most little girls at some point dream of living in a fairy tale. The big surprise when we grow up is not that the fairy tale was a myth but that it is far more dangerous than we thought. We do live in a fairy tale, but it often seems as if both the dragon and the wicked witch are winning. Things are not what they were meant to be. Fire and ice. Beauty and terror. Pain and healing. We came into this life gasping for air, and we are gasping still.

A great darkness of the world is misogyny—the hatred of women. We see stories of violence, prejudice, and neglect from every country, including our own.

We experience misogyny ourselves in both dramatic and subtle ways.

When Jesus came onto the scene, he turned misogyny on its head. A rabbi at that time wouldn't speak to a woman in public, not even his own wife (this is still true for orthodox rabbis). Even today an orthodox Jewish man is forbidden to touch or be touched by any woman who is not his wife or a close family relation. Jesus didn't abide by those rules. During his ministry Jesus engaged with women many times. He spoke to them. He touched them. He taught them. He esteemed them. He allowed women to minister to him physically, touching him, washing his feet, anointing him with oil and with their tears. Female disciples traveled with him, supported him, learned from him, and sat at his feet. If the church, the body of Christ, had followed the example Jesus set instead of the traditions of men held captive to sin and the fall, we would have a much higher history here.

The good news is that Life has already won out. Love has won out. Yes, we remain on the battlefield, in the middle of a world that often demeans and hurts women. But God loves women. Jesus loves women. And as we become more ourselves, we come to love who we are as women and recognize all we have to offer a broken world.

Jesus, thank you for your love for women in a world that does not always love us. Even in the midst of this battle, help me live with love, not bitterness. Bless my femininity so that I might know you more! Amen.

18

---

more than conquerors

*For our struggle is not against flesh and blood, but
against the rulers, against the authorities, against
the powers of this dark world and against the
spiritual forces of evil in the heavenly realms.*
—Ephesians 6:12

The source of evil against women in this world is
not men, not the church, not even governments or
systems of injustice. Scripture makes it clear that the
source of evil is the Evil One himself. If we blame
anything else, nothing will change.

Jesus called Satan the prince of this world. Satan
is the prince of darkness, whose sole aim is to steal,
kill, and destroy life in all its forms. He has power
here on earth, wherever the kingdom of God is not
being enforced or advanced. He is the source of the
hatred of women, the hatred you have endured. But
let us remember: Jesus has won all victory through his

crucifixion, resurrection, and ascension. All authority in heaven and on earth was given back to him, where it rightly belongs. And then Jesus gave it to us.

When we come to understand that Satan is the cause of hatred against women, we can not only make leaps forward in understanding our lives but also find our way through the battle to the goodness God has for us and the goodness he wants to bring through us.

There is a reason the Enemy fears women and has poured his hatred onto our very existence. Let him be afraid, then. We are more than conquerors through Christ who strengthens us, and we will not be overcome. God is our strength. Jesus is our defender. The Holy Spirit is our portion. And in the name of our God and Savior, we will choose to love him. We will choose to bow down in surrendered worship to our God. And by the power of Christ in us, we will choose to rise up and be women of God, bringing his kingdom in unyielding and merciful strength.

Father God, I repent of any hatred of women that has taken root in my heart. Hatred of women is hatred of

myself and not from you. I choose to embrace my woman-
hood. I thank you for my life, and I choose life. I give my
life fully to you now, Jesus, and I invite you to have your
way in me. I pray all of this in your glorious and beautiful
name, Jesus Christ. Amen.

19

---

coheirs with Christ

We are hard pressed on every side, but not crushed;
perplexed, but not in despair; persecuted, but not
abandoned; struck down, but not destroyed.
—2 Corinthians 4:8–9

Just as we cannot overcome our feminine bodies by hating them, we cannot overcome misogyny by hating women, or men. When we hate women, we hate ourselves. When we diminish the role of women, we diminish ourselves. When we are jealous or envious, slandering other women, we join the Enemy's assault on them. In doing those things we come into agreement with the Enemy of our hearts and of God by saying that what God has made is *not* good.

It's time to stop doing that. The way to navigate the battle begins with love. Not blame, not finger-pointing, but love.

Let us begin by celebrating the role we play. Let us champion these callings and celebrate them every way we can. The truth is that who we are as women, what we bring, and the role we play in the world, in the kingdom of God, and in the lives of men, women, and children are of immeasurable worth and power.

The kingdom of God will not advance as it needs to without women rising up and playing their role. The transformation and healing of a man requires the presence, strength, and mercy of a woman. Men will not become the men they are meant to be without godly women pouring into their lives. Women will not become who they are meant to be without the strength, encouragement, and wisdom of other women nurturing their lives. Women are image bearers of God. Women are coheirs with Christ. Women are valued, worthy, powerful, and needed.

Yes, it's been hard. But that's because you are so vitally needed. Your valiant feminine heart is needed today in the lives of those you live with, work with, and love.

God, thank you for creating women with a unique and vital role in this world. How are you calling me to use my gifts and power as a woman today?

20

beautiful girl

As a mother comforts her child,
so will I comfort you.
—Isaiah 66:13

Our mothers have blessed and wounded us. Looking at our relationships with our mothers is part of finding the healing Jesus has for us on our journey of realizing we are beautiful now.

Mothers have the ability to withhold acceptance, value, love. Our mothers failed us when, without meaning to, they passed on low self-esteem to us. Or based our self-worth on anything other than the fact that we exist.

God does not do that. Our worth is not based on what we do, which life path we choose, or what we believe. Our worth is inherent in the fact that we are image bearers of the living God.

If we were not of great worth, then the blood of goats and lambs, oxen and bulls would have been enough to purchase humanity out of captivity. Back in the garden of Eden, you remember, the human race went into captivity, and the price to buy us back was so high that no ransom note was even sent. But God knew and pursued us. He intervened.

Let God continue to mother you, to heal you. Continue to pray and press in toward the more that God has for you. And know that, whether she ever conveyed it to you or not, you were a *gift* to your mother's heart. Every mother learns more from her children than she ever teaches them.

You were a beautiful little girl who was deeply loved, a beautiful little girl who had a heavenly Parent who delighted in her, grieved with her, and worked in her life even in unseen ways. Beautiful then. Beautiful now.

How has your mother's view of herself, her body, and her role as a woman affected your view of yourself?

21

---

healing memories

I will repay you for the years the locusts have eaten.
—Joel 2:25

What you received from your mother is formative and foundational, but where it was not good, it does not have to be your destiny. The healing presence of Jesus Christ can come in and wash clean the pain of your childhood. What *you* believe, what *you* choose now is your path and your future.

Jesus is the one who has the right to speak into our lives with authority and power. He has the power to bless who we are and who we are becoming. He is our inheritance, and we must bring him our hearts, our wounds, all that we were meant to have as girls growing up. His name is Faithful and True. He is the same yesterday, today, and forever. He wants to heal us!

When we go back and remember the wounds of our childhood, the events themselves do not change, but in the light of Jesus's love and presence, we can view and experience them differently. The sting of death is removed, the pain of the memory is released to Jesus, and healing comes. God will actually reframe our history and memories as he heals us. As God nurtures, protects, prepares, and initiates us, he restores us to the truth of who we are and the reality of the life we are living and are meant to live. We *are* loved, wanted, seen, delighted in, provided for, cherished, chosen, known, and planned on. We are set apart, believed in, invited, valued, of immeasurable worth, and blessed.

Holy Trinity, I invoke your healing presence now. Come and meet me here. I sanctify my memories and my imagination to you, God. I ask you to come and to reveal where I need healing, Jesus, and I ask you to heal me. Where do you want to come, God? Where do I need you to come? Is it while I was in the womb? Is it as a child, a little girl, a young woman? Is it to every stage of my life? Come, Jesus. I ask you to come for me and to heal me in the deep places and unseen realms of my heart. I need you. Come with your light and your love. Come with your tender, strong, and merciful presence and fill me here. In Jesus's name, amen.

22

invite Jesus here

He spoke the word that healed you.
—Psalm 107:20 MSG

When you choose to pray for healing from your past, Jesus will show you memories and events and bring back feelings that you had. Were you satisfied as a child? Were your basic needs—for food, safety, and healthy touch—met? Did you receive the attention you needed? Were you celebrated simply because you existed as yourself?

Linger, and invite Jesus here.

Jesus, my healer, help me remember what needs to be remembered. Thank you for loving the child I was and for loving the woman I am today.

As Jesus reveals things to you, invite him in, ask him to heal. Is forgiveness needed? Forgive. Are tears needed? Allow those tears to come, but invite Jesus into those tears as you do. Ask for his healing. Ask him to nurture you in this very place.

Linger, and then continue with this prayer as you invite Jesus here.

Jesus, my healer, come to me when I cry. I want to forgive; help me do so.

A mother is supposed to know what is going on in her child's life. To be aware. To intervene. Did your mother notice? Did she intervene? Did she protect?

Invite Jesus here.

Jesus, my healer, come into my need for protection. Come into the places that needed protection when I was a child. Show me where I need healing.

A mother encourages her daughter toward independence and self-confidence. As a child, were you accepted? Were you seen? Celebrated? Were you encouraged to pursue your interests? Did you receive attention and delight? Do you remember receiving encouragement to become your unique self? Were you initiated into the feminine world with approval and a sense of belonging?

Invite Jesus here.

Jesus, my healer, come into my need for encourage-ment, my desire for my true self to be celebrated.

I've seen in my own story how God can heal a painful past. Abuse. Alcoholism. Self-hatred. As hard as the process can be, the freedom, healing, and joy that come make it worth it.

Jesus, come. Show me where I need healing.

23

God's lullaby

*He'll calm you with his love
and delight you with his songs.*
—Zephaniah 3:17 MSG

Several years ago John and I escaped the freezing temperatures of a Colorado winter to visit friends in Tucson. After a restful day exploring the wonder of the desert, we gathered together for evening prayer. A phrase of one friend's prayer caught my imagination: "Father, sing your lullaby of delight over us."

As many mothers do, I used to make up songs for my children, singing lullabies softly to coax my young sons to sleep. Never remembering the correct words, I made them up as I went along, inserting their names often. I loved it. Turns out, they loved it too.

As I laid me down to sleep that night in Tucson, I asked God what his lullaby of delight over me sounded like. My mind immediately flashed to holy moments from earlier in the day: sitting alone in the shade, listening to the wind blow through the leaves of the eucalyptus trees towering above me, the sound like water, like the movement of life. I remembered the sound of the red-tailed hawks crying and calling to each other as they circled above their nearby nest. The song of quails and mourning doves and birds I didn't recognize added their melodies—a living symphony. Then all was quiet again save for the movement of leaves as another rolling breeze sang its way through the swaying trees.

A holy song. A lullaby of delight. Sung over me. Singing over you.

What is God's lullaby to you today? Close your eyes and imagine God singing over you. What are the words? What do you feel when you hear his voice?

24

---

the only reflection
that matters

How beautiful you are, my darling!
Oh, how beautiful!
Your eyes behind your veil are doves.
—Song of Songs 4:1

My mother used to say, "Beauty before pain!"—meaning, being beautiful is more important than not feeling terrible. High heels with our toes pinched into the pointy tip. Spanx. Waxing. Trimming. Plucking. Paying.

Maybe that's why I spend far too much time in front of a well-lit magnifying mirror, criticizing my skin, my face, and those horrible chin hairs that seem to come from nowhere. My husband encourages me to throw out that mirror. Maybe I'll be ready when I've attained a hair-free status. Or better, maybe I'll throw it away when my soul more fully embraces the truth of what God says about me.

The truth is, God has been inviting me to throw the magnifying mirror away for years. He has been inviting me to be free from gazing at the multiple imperfections in my face and in my soul and instead to believe the reflection he is showing me.

The only reflection that really matters is the reflection we see in God's loving and joyous eyes. What does he see? What does he say? He says we are beautiful *now*.

How do you see me today, Jesus? When you look at me closely, when you study me, what do you see? Help me see myself as you do.

25

Jesus is the goal

There has never been the slightest doubt in my
mind that the God who started this great work in
you would keep at it and bring it to a flourishing
finish on the very day Christ Jesus appears.
—Philippians 1:6 MSG

Perfection in any vital area of our life is not going to happen. There, I said it. Now we can improve. We can grow. We can become more loving, more grace filled, more merciful. We are no longer bound to sin, slaves to its din of temptation. We are still going to sin. But we don't *have* to. The secret is Jesus.

Jesus is inviting us to relax in the beauty he has bestowed upon us. He wants us to cease striving to attain a level of perfection that looks wonderful on a doll or on a magazine cover but is not attainable in the living, breathing realm of humanity.

Think about it: God does not tell us that the goal is perfection on earth. The media, our critical inner voices, and envy tell us to keep striving for perfection. But our hope doesn't rest on our finally getting it together. Our hope rests in Jesus. Jesus in us. It's Christ in us, the hope of glory. We won't be perfect on this side of heaven. But Jesus is perfect. Always. We are becoming more holy and true. Jesus already is. His name isn't "Becoming." It is "I Am." Perfection isn't the goal. Jesus is.

Jesus, thank you for not calling me to be perfect today! You are calling me to be yours.

26

God loves quirky

For we are God's handiwork, created in Christ Jesus to do good works, which God prepared in advance for us to do.
—Ephesians 2:10

People are weird. Well, I'm not—but everyone else is. The definition of *normal* for most of us is "me." It is actually helpful to acknowledge the truth that we are just as quirky as everyone else and that God loves quirky! He loves you! He has a fabulous sense of humor, and he adores yours. (He always gets your jokes even if no one else does!)

He made you *you*—on purpose. Becoming ourselves means we are actively cooperating with God's intention for our lives, not fighting him or ourselves. God accepts us right at this moment, and he wants us to accept ourselves as well. He looks at us with pleasure and with mercy, and he wants us to look at ourselves with pleasure and mercy too! Accepting who we are includes accepting and being thankful for our imperfect bodies, but it isn't limited to that. We can accept other truths about ourselves.

Our personality is our own. Our story is our own. Our taste is our own. The way we have chosen to self-protect is ours. We have a style of relating, a kind of sin we easily fall prey to, and a favorite way to spend a free afternoon. We already are ourselves. Unique. After all, cookie cutters only work well for cookies.

Jesus, I want to actively cooperate with your intention for my life. You accept me right now, and I want to accept myself too. How do you want me to be myself today?

27

---

embracing God's good work

For you created my inmost being;
you knit me together in my mother's womb.
I praise you because I am fearfully
and wonderfully made;
your works are wonderful,
I know that full well.
—Psalm 139:13–14

God not only accepts us, he embraces us. Embracing ourselves is a stretch for most of us, but consider: Jesus commands us to love our neighbor as we love ourselves. How can we love our neighbor as ourselves if we do not love ourselves? How can we become joyful women if we are unable to see the humor in our own folly? We do become even more ourselves as we repent of sin in our lives, but God does not live in a perpetual state of disappointment over who we are. Berating ourselves for our flaws and our weaknesses only undermines our strength to become.

Repenting from our sin is essential.

Beating ourselves up for sinning is no longer an option.

Embracing ourselves has nothing to do with arrogance or settling for a lower version of who we are. Embracing ourselves has everything to do with embracing the goodness of God's creative work in us. It means trusting God, believing that all he has made is glorious and good. And that includes us. You are the only one who can be you. The world, the kingdom of God, and all those around you need you to embrace who you are created to be as you become more fully your *true* self.

Dear beautiful God, you take my breath away. It is too amazing for me to grasp that I take yours away too! I remember now that though man looks at the outward appearance, you look at the heart. My heart is yours. You gave me a new one when I trusted in Jesus, and my heart is beautiful to you. Help me believe it, Father. Help me rest in it. In Jesus's name.

28

---

a higher truth

But me he caught—reached all the way
from sky to sea; he pulled me out
of that ocean of hate, that enemy chaos,
the void in which I was drowning.
They hit me when I was down,
but GOD stuck by me.
He stood me up on a wide-open field;
I stood there saved—surprised to be loved!
—Psalm 18:16–19 MSG

Oops. The scale said what? Okay. Breathe. It is information. Only information. It is not judgment. It might feel like it is, but it is not. Yes, perhaps we need to drink more water and pay attention to what we are eating and make more mindful and healthy choices. That would be good. But the number is only a number. The mirror is only a mirror. The opinions of others are simply their own opinions. How much we weigh, what we wear, and what others think of us don't have anything to do with who we *are*.

You have a higher truth to look to today. You have been bought with a price; you are not your own. You are holy and dearly loved. You are pursued and fought for—*today*. You can focus on the number on the scale or the number in the bank account or at a myriad of other numbers, *or* you can focus on the number of times God thinks of you, plans for you, fights for you, longs for you. Oh, wait. You can't count that high. The One who counts the hairs on your head and catches your every tear and knows every day of your life thinks you are beautiful *now*. Rest in that, beloved one. And enter your day with confidence and joy. You are his.

Oh, God, THANK YOU for interjecting your truth into my thoughts! I love how you think of me!

29

risk dreaming

Abraham never wavered in believing God's
promise. In fact, his faith grew stronger,
and in this he brought glory to God.
—Romans 4:20 NLT

According to David Kohl, professor emeritus at Virginia
Tech, people who regularly write down their dreams and
desires earn nine times as much over their lifetimes as
people who don't. (Think of what you could do with
that! What good could you bring? What ministry could
you support?) Life dreams come true for people who
allow themselves to dream, who own their dreams, and
who write them down and look at them periodically.

Sixteen percent of Americans say they have
dreams but don't write them down. Four percent have
dreams and desires, and write them down, but less than
1 percent review and update them on a regular basis.
But most Americans (80 percent) say they don't have

any dreams, and we can imagine why. Life can suck the dreaming right out of you. The living God wants to pour those dreams back in.

I encourage you to risk dreaming and writing your dreams down. Once you get started, you'll find there are things you want. And if you can't get started, another approach is to begin listing the things you like. From the fragrance of lilacs to a cozy blanket in front of a fire to laughing with friends, it's nourishing to become aware of what you enjoy and to write it down.

It's good to sit with God in the quiet and ask him, *What do I want?* and *What do you want for me?*

Does it feel dangerous to dream? Risky to hope? Consider this: We can't out-give God. We can't out-love him, and we can't out-dream him. Give yourself permission to dream big! Dream deep. Dream wide.

Nothing is impossible with God. Nothing is too good to be true. After all, if you don't have a dream, how can you have a dream come true?

Jesus, come. Guide me. Holy Spirit, fill me. Dream with me and in me. Help me to unlock the desires you have planted in my heart and to write them down. Help me dream big.

30

---

wanting what God wants

But seek first his kingdom and his righteousness,
and all these things will be given to you as well.
—Matthew 6:33

I have dreams today that are large and varied. On my list are things like: I want to grow tomatoes in a pot and make an amazing *tres leches* cake. I want to be able to get on a horse without using a block. There are people I want to see come to Christ, countries I want to travel to and minister in, and a size I want to wear.

I have longings and dreams for my husband and for my sons and for our relationships. I want to learn to take really good pictures and capture the beauty that captures my eye. I want to be strong. I want to know the heart of God intimately. I want his life to fill me and flow through me powerfully and joyfully. I want to find out how deeply I can dive into the vastness of his love—how much of his heart can I know?

Some dreams come true here, on this side of heaven. As in, I'm pretty sure that one day I am going to be able to grow tomatoes. And there are some that will simply continue to unfold, like really knowing the heart of God.

I love looking at my list of dreams because it reveals something about who God created me to be. Even my "smaller" dreams about baking and gardening remind me that God made me in his image as a creator, and when I create, I draw closer to him. God is so good to give us joy in what he wants for us already!

Dearest Father, I believe you are good and reward those who seek you, but I get confused by the place of my dreams. I don't want to chase after my own happiness but after what would give you glory and pleasure. Still, I know I matter to you and that you gave me these desires for a reason. May they lead me deeper into your heart this day as I lay them down at your feet. I trust you to guide me. I choose not to kill my dreams but to trust you with them. With hope and in Jesus's name.

31

---

a tender heart

And I will give you a new heart, and I will put a new spirit in you. I will take out your stony, stubborn heart and give you a tender, responsive heart.
—Ezekiel 36:26 NLT

I encourage you to keep your heart open and continue writing down your dreams. Keep asking God to show you more and more of his dreams and desires for you. I do know that one of the things he wants is for your heart to become more alive, more awake, and more aware of your own inner workings and his pleasure over who you are. Today. Right in this moment. *Who you are* fleshes out in *what you want.*

Awakening and owning the dreams that God has placed in our hearts isn't about getting stuff or attaining something. It's not about asking for what we need. He's already promised to supply our needs. It's about embracing who we are and who he has created us to be.

In him. He is our dream come true, and the one true love of our life. But we can't love him with our whole hearts when our hearts are asleep. To love Jesus means to risk coming awake, to risk wanting and desiring. It means risking that you believe one day your dreams may come true.

Ask yourself: *What would I love to do? What would I love to experience or create or offer? What do I want to be really good at? What do I want with God? What does God want with me? What do I want to be known for?* Write down your answers to these questions. Ask God to shape your dreams and help you be expectant for him to make your dreams come true.

32

living life on purpose

I'm not saying that I have this all together, that I have it made. But I am well on my way, reaching out for Christ, who has so wondrously reached out for me.
—Philippians 3:12 MSG

Writing down your dreams and desires can be just between you and God. You can share your dreams with someone in your life who you know will handle your heart well, but you don't have to. Let your want-o-meter go off the charts. It is not even remotely connected to your dissatisfied-o-meter.

You have the desires you do for a reason. Some desires you share with many others. Many people want the same core, good things: a community, a relationship, a deeper walk with God. But many of your dreams and desires are yours alone. God has given them to you to awaken to, embrace, nurture, pursue, and then offer.

Let God use your dreams to guide you into the fuller expression of your unfolding glorious self!

We need to live increasingly from the fullness of our whole hearts in order to become who we are meant to be and play the significant role that is ours to play. We want to be awake and alert. We want to be women who *live their lives on purpose.*

God gives us our dreams, and we give them back to him. By dreaming and writing them down, we aren't demanding they come true. We are just owning the reality that they are a part of us. And since they are a part of us, we embrace them.

Jesus, come. Lead me. Help me capture on paper the desires you have planted in my heart. Help me embrace the dreams you have for me. Guide me into the fuller expression of the woman you want me to be.

33

---

inhabiting your beauty

For everything created by God is good.
—1 Timothy 4:4 ESV

A few years ago I came home from a hair appointment, and honestly my hair looked fantastic. I don't know what my hairdresser does, but the day she does my hair, it's amazing. I can never replicate it. On this particular day I looked in the mirror and saw fabulous hair, and I felt pretty. I *felt* pretty. We all know that can be a rare occurrence!

I had a meeting to go to in a couple of hours, so I changed into more work-appropriate attire: a pair of nicer jeans. I love these jeans. I don't know what it is about them, but they work. I put on a red top and big turquoise earrings. Not my usual go-to outfit, but I loved it.

As soon as I was dressed, a friend dropped by unexpectedly, and when she saw me, she stopped dead in her tracks and exclaimed, "You are inhabiting your beauty!"

I was inhabiting my beauty. I had worn the jeans before, the top before, and probably the earrings with them, but something in my spirit had relaxed and I was embracing being myself, a woman who believed God when he said, "You are lovely."

I wasn't squeezing into the pants by the use of an elastic torture device, nor was I squeezing my soul into any other prescribed form. Rather, I was inhabiting my beauty, just being me and embracing who that is. It might have been for the first time, but please, Jesus, not for the last.

Some reading this may say, "Those jeans must be amazing and looked really great on you, but I don't look good in any pair of jeans." Can I just tell you that those jeans are a size 24? Those fabulous, awesome, man-I-love-these-pants are a size 24.

I am no longer a size 24, but I pray to inhabit my beauty as well as I did on that monumental day. On every level.

God, I love that you live in me. YOUR beauty is in ME. How can I let your light shine through my physical body today?

34

a shining light

The righteous will flourish like a palm tree,
they will grow like a cedar in Lebanon;
planted in the house of the LORD;
they will flourish in the courts of our God.
They will still bear fruit in old age,
they will stay fresh and green.
—Psalm 92:12–14

A couple of years ago, I was at a church luncheon for the women's ministry, and one table was filled with older women. Two were ninety, and one was celebrating her ninety-third birthday that very day. Their hair was coiffed, their makeup applied, their clothes bright and dressy. They were having so much fun that I just wanted to be at their table.

To say that our beauty as women peaks somewhere in our twenties is laughably absurd. Yes, there is a vibrant beauty to youth, but *these* women—these much older women—were stunning. They had wrinkles and gray hair. No Botox or lip filler or liposuction could erase their years. But they had something else much more beautiful than youth. They had hearts that had been cultivated by faith over decades.

To our great loss, in our society we no longer value the wisdom and expertise that comes through living well through many years. We forget that silver hair and wrinkles are earned. Yet God says our latter glory will exceed our former. When I think about who I will be in the decades ahead, I realize what I want most of all is for God's love to radiate from me.

The women I met that day had a light shining from their eyes that all the sorrow and pain and loss they had undoubtedly endured could not extinguish. They loved God and their hearts were alive. Nothing is more gorgeous than that.

Thank you, Lord, for the older women in my life who reflect your beauty and your faithfulness. May I continue to learn from them, and may I be a model for those who are younger. Amen.

a quality of spirit

Has anyone by fussing in front of the mirror ever
gotten taller by so much as an inch? All this time and
money wasted on fashion—do you think it makes that
much difference? Instead of looking at the fashions,
walk out into the fields and look at the wildflowers.
They never primp or shop, but have you ever seen color
and design quite like it? The ten best-dressed men and
women in the country look shabby alongside them.
—Matthew 6:27–29 MSG

I have learned that being beautiful, feeling lovely, and
enjoying who we are have absolutely nothing to do
with our weight, our age, or the shape of our bodies.
Take that in for a moment and try it on for size. Let the
possibility of that being true settle into your spirit for
a moment before you quickly dismiss the idea. Beauty
is not about the hair, the clothes, the marital status,
the bank account, or the number on the scale. Being

beautiful is a quality of spirit recognized primarily in a woman whose soul is at rest because she believes her God when he calls her lovely. She is no longer striving to reach the world's unattainable standards of beauty and acceptance but instead is receiving the inheritance that is hers as an image bearer of the living God. She is embracing who God has made her to be.

You are a stunner. And the more you grow in knowing God, the more you will love him, and the more his life and his beauty will inhabit you and flow out from your unique, fabulous, embraceable self.

Go ahead and take a good long look in the mirror. Tell yourself you are a knockout. God says you are, and, well, he ought to know.

Lord, thank you! May you shine on and through those I love, and also on and through me. I love you!

36

---

live boldly

*There is no fear in love. But perfect love drives
out fear, because fear has to do with punishment.
The one who fears is not made perfect in love.*
—1 John 4:18

One night when I was in college, I came home alone
to my dark apartment, unlocked the door, walked in,
and slammed it shut behind me. After I took several
steps, I began to feel that something was off. I looked
back, and in the shadows behind the door, shrouded
by the night, was a man. I didn't scream. I didn't run.
I didn't even move. My legs turned into Jell-O and I
collapsed onto the floor. Great to know what I do in
a life-threatening situation. I've always been a little
disappointed by my petrified reaction. Still, fear will
do that to a person. (The man turned out to be my
roommate's boyfriend playing a joke on me. And yes,
he felt terrible about it.)

In that moment when fear gripped me, I was utterly powerless. Have you ever had those awful dreams where you need to cry out to save someone or to save yourself—and for the life of you, you can't utter a sound? Or you need to get away, but your legs feel frozen and you cannot move, cannot run?

Fear paralyzes. Fear in its mildest, tamest form is a party pooper. It is a wet blanket that smothers the fiery passion God deposited in your heart when he formed you. Fear freezes us into inaction. Frozen ideas, frozen souls, frozen bodies can't move, can't dream, can't risk, can't love, and can't live. Fear chains us.

No wonder Scripture tells us that fear and love can never go together. When we live in fear, we are not free to love others, God, or ourselves as God intended. Our spirits slump to the floor the way I did all those years ago!

Embracing God's love for us empowers us to live boldly, without fear, free to be who God created us to be.

Jesus, come and uproot my fear. Replace it with a revelation of your goodness. Overwhelm my fear with your

love. Come into the gap in my soul between what I pro-
fess to believe and what I truly do. I want to know you.
Deeply. Truly. In the way that lends itself to so easily trust
you. Come for me again, oh Faithful Friend.

37

---

what will God say?

The fear of the LORD is the beginning of wisdom.
—Proverbs 9:10

Fear is defined as *a vital response to physical and emotional danger*. If we were unable to feel fear, we wouldn't protect ourselves from legitimate threats. So fear can have its place. After all, God doesn't want us living a fantasy life or a life of denying reality.

God also wants us to live a life where we continually grow in wisdom, which comes from fearing God. So there is a good fear, a holy fear, a fear that makes you want to honor and do homage to the One who deserves it.

The fear that gets us into the most trouble is not fearing God, but fearing people. This is a fear we are all well acquainted with. The fear of looking or sounding stupid and then being dismissed, expelled, shunned. That's the fear known to every elementary, middle school, and high school student alive. But do we ever really get over that? This is the same fear that keeps us silent when we would be better off speaking. It's the fear of going against the grain or saying what the Holy Spirit prompts us to say.

Fear in its most wicked, powerful form cripples our souls and warps the very fabric of our hearts. It reshapes our inner reality until we bear no resemblance to the dream that is us, to who we *really* are. And our lives bear no resemblance to the lives we are meant to be living. Fear robs us of our very selves.

As we embrace the truth that we are beautiful now, safe in God's arms, our question changes from, "What will man say?" to "What will God say?" We realize that we would rather trust God's loving response to us than any erratic response of man. So if you are looking for wisdom in life, take heart. This transformation is where wisdom begins.

Are you saying yes to anything in your life today out of fear, rather than out of love?

38

---

losing ourselves

The fear of man lays a snare.
—Proverbs 29:25 ESV

Some people define F.E.A.R. as False Evidence Appearing Real. Yet often the evidence that appears real *is* real. There may be a man standing behind the door. There are car accidents. Horrible, tragic things do happen. And you may never see them coming until they are upon you. You know this personally. And you can quickly put two and two together: If such tragedy could befall that family, who knows what could happen to ours? If *this* bad thing can happen, then *that* even worse thing could happen too.

Women are particularly vulnerable to fears of all kinds because we care, because we love, because in God's gracious design we are vulnerable and gloriously so. Our vulnerability is part of what makes us women; it enables us to love as we do, to protect relationships as we do, to comfort and offer mercy, to bring a creative eye to the world. And yes, it also makes us vulnerable to fear.

That means we are swift on our feet when it comes to running down trails of fear and speculation. Say you have a recurring headache. How quickly do you jump to, *Maybe it's a brain tumor. Maybe I'm dying?* Your best friend doesn't call for several days. You start thinking, *She's mad at me. I offended her. She's probably talking with someone else now. I've been replaced.* Most of my friends confess to this. I confess to it! Fear changes a beautiful part of us—vulnerable, loving, creative—into something that paralyzes our true selves.

Jesus, my imagination, love for others, and vulnerability are all good gifts—yet when fear gets in the way, those good gifts get twisted and I hurt myself and others. I don't want to fall into the snare of fear. Redeem these gifts so that I can use them as you intended, not as a doorway to worry. Amen.

39

out of control

Do not give way to fear.
—1 Peter 3:6

In order to overcome fear, we first have to be honest about life on this planet.

We fear that our marriage will not last. It may not. We fear that we may lose something or someone precious to us, and we may. We fear being embarrassed if we speak up or fall down or come out of the bathroom trailing toilet paper. Things happen. Little things. Huge things. We fear failure in life, failure *at* life.

The truth is, on any given day, we do not know what is coming our way. We are living in a fallen world and we are women who love. When you love someone, you risk losing them. You risk enduring every painful thing we'd much rather avoid. Like many women, my deepest fear is that something terrible will happen to my husband or my sons. What is yours?

The hard, true thing about our deepest fears is that what happens is completely out of our control. Life is out of our control. People are out of our control, and certainly their choices are out of our control. We can ultimately choose life for only one person. Ourselves. How does that truth change your thoughts and fears about today?

Jesus, I do not know what will happen in my life or in the news today or tomorrow or any day after that. I recognize that the future is out of my control. But my thoughts and fears are within my control. Help me lay them at your feet, again and again. In Jesus's name, amen.

40

God's greatest command

For the Spirit God gave does not make us timid,
but gives us power, love and self-discipline.
—2 Timothy 1:7

Fear can be a motivator. But it is never an agent of lasting change. Fear of having no friends, for instance, can cause you to be less self-centered or to listen more. Fear of being stuck personally can prompt you to see a counselor. Fear of being stuck professionally can push you to take a class or seek a mentor. Fear can motivate in good ways, such as an adrenaline rush causing you to run for safety.

But fear is just the catalyst. It is not an agent of change any more than shame is. If we get stuck in fear, rather than letting it urge us on and then leaving it behind, we can't grow. If unaddressed, fear will simply attempt to make peace with us. "It's *normal* to be afraid of this or that. It's *fine*. If you stop being afraid, something bad will happen." Once it has a hold on a certain area of your life, fear will do its best to increase its hold on more places.

You know what we do as women when we feel afraid: we tell ourselves that we can control a situation, a person, or a relationship if we simply protect it. If something bad happens, it's our fault, so we better always be on guard—in other words, we better always be fearful.

That's a lie. When we spend our days and our energies trying to protect ourselves, rather than trusting God, we get stuck in our journey of becoming.

God is a God of love, and he commands us to *love*—not to fear and not to play mind games all day under the illusion of control. He commands us to love.

Today I choose to love, not to fear. They cannot go together.

41

can we trust God?

You are good, and what you do is good.
—Psalm 119:68

I'm a mother. My life and my heart are out running around hither and yon completely out of my control. I have risk-taking, adventure-loving, passionate sons who prefer cliff jumping to stamp collecting, motorcycles to minivans, and rock climbing to studying coins. I am aware of the world we live in, both the physical and spiritual realities. I am acquainted with fear. Too many times I have tried to ease my fears by reaching for control over my husband, my sons, and my world. It almost always made things worse.

I once got a call from a friend asking me for advice about her relationship with her teenage son. He had recently said to her, "You need to back off." Her husband later told her, "You have your foot on his throat." She was trying to control him. Pushing him to talk. Bringing up the subjects of drugs and alcohol and safety and godliness again and again and again. She wasn't inviting him to conversation but demanding that he listen. Out of—you guessed it—fear. She wanted to keep him close and safe. It was having the opposite effect. She learned that through her fear-based actions, she was pushing him away.

Parameters are good. Conversations are good. Instruction is good. We are right to control our children and teach them about safety and choices and the world in which they live and, as they mature, to give them increasing amounts of freedom. We lengthen the leash that's attached to our hip and then let it go. And when we can't do that, the issue is fear. But the deeper issue is *trust*.

Can we trust our lives, our futures, and the lives of those we love to God? Can we trust a God we can't control? Can we trust this God whose take on life and death and suffering and joy is so very different from our own?

Yes. Yes, we can.

Because we know him. And we know he is good.

Jesus, you are good. I trust you with my life today. I trust you with the lives of those I love. So often my love for others leads me to intense fear and worry. What do I do with those thoughts and feelings? How do I trust you when I am so out of control? Help me understand what it means today that you are a good God. In Jesus's name, amen.

42

---

the only safe place

In peace I will lie down and sleep,
for you alone, LORD,
make me dwell in safety.
—Psalm 4:8

On our way to becoming ourselves, we have to choose life. Choose risk. Choose love. The only safe place for our hearts is to dive deeply into the magnificent, eternal, ridiculous, overwhelming love that God has for us. His love is the only safety net that will hold. Doesn't that sound better than a life of fearful, false control? Come and be free in the love of God.

I'm not making idle religious promises here. Becoming a Christian does not mean that we will be safe from tragedy, loss, or sorrow. But it does mean that in it and through it, *we will be all right*. Actually, we will be much better than all right. Though we don't have all the control and assurance we may want, we as God's beloved can be certain of many things.

For one thing, we can be pretty sure we are going to die. But we don't need to fear it because we can be certain of what is coming next. Eternal life is real. Heaven is real. Some of those we love deeply have already gone on before us, and the pain of losing them is comforted by the fact that we have not lost them forever. We are parted now for a little while. A sweet reunion is coming. We are promised that.

Jesus also promises that he will never leave us or forsake us. That's true no matter what our emotions or circumstances are telling us.

We know that we are more than conquerors through him who loves us. We know that nothing, nothing, *nothing* will be able to separate us from the love of God that is in Christ Jesus our Lord. And we know that in all things God works for the good of those who love him, who have been called according to his purpose. All things. Even the other shoe dropping.

Now that's a promise to hold on to.

I have been called according to God's purpose. Nothing I fear can ever change that truth!

43

all your needs

*And my God will meet all your needs according
to the riches of his glory in Christ Jesus.*
—Philippians 4:19

Fear tells us in the morning: *You don't have enough
energy or time or love to get through today.* Fear tells us
at the grocery store: *You'll never have enough money to
make it to payday.* Fear tells us in the middle of the
night: *If God really loved you, you would have more.*

God promises that we will have everything we
need. *Everything.* Our needs won't be met according
to the destitution of the world or to the poverty of our
own faith in the moment but according to the riches in
Jesus. There's no one richer than him!

Now, I admit that what I believe I need doesn't
always line up with what God believes I need. But all
of us have stories of God coming through when we
needed him most. From groceries left on my doorstep,

to an anonymous gift of twenty dollars that allowed me to put gas in my car, to the tuition for college supplied on the date it was due, I have amazing stories.

Satan uses our needs to separate us from God when we question God's goodness and give in to fear. God uses our needs to draw us closer to him when we learn to depend on him and expect his provision. Who are you going to believe today?

Jesus, these are my needs today, big and small. [Tell him your needs.] *I believe you will meet my needs according to your abundant love for me!*

44

fearless

"They will fight against you but will not overcome you, for I am with you and will rescue you," declares the LORD.
—Jeremiah 1:19

Our God is a God of deliverance. But his view is different from ours. Jeremiah was set apart in his mother's womb to be a prophet. That promise was fulfilled many times in the biblical narrative. But Jeremiah was attacked by his own brothers, beaten and put into the stocks by a priest and false prophet, imprisoned by the king, threatened with death, thrown into a cistern by Judah's officials, and opposed by a false prophet.

Ummmm. When did God rescue him exactly? After he was beaten. After he was imprisoned. After he was threatened, opposed, and thrown into a cistern. Yes, God's view is dramatically different from ours. Jeremiah went through much travail. So has every saint before him and after him, though not all to that extreme. Just as God told Jeremiah, he tells us, "Don't be afraid." He says, "My grace is sufficient for you."

A friend recently shared this wisdom: "Love displaces fear, so in order to truly become so fearless that you can live out the way of life God has for you, you will have to become so immersed in the presence of love that there is no room for fear. Courage comes from love, never from fear."

The kingdom of God is advancing, and the gates of hell will not prevail against it. Don't you want to advance along with it? Don't you want to help it to advance? And don't you want to advance into the deeper realms of the heart of God? Advance into more healing, more deliverance, more intimacy, more life? Fear makes us retreat. Love causes us to move forward to further the kingdom of God.

Jesus, how do you want me to advance with the kingdom of God today? How are you drawing me deeper into your heart?

45

one of his own

Your faith has healed you. Go in peace.
—Mark 5:34

Jesus was on a mission to save the life of a man's daughter. A crowd went with him. He was being jostled, pushed against, pressed into when suddenly he stopped and asked, "Who touched me?"

A woman came forward. She fell at his feet and told him the whole story. She had been bleeding for twelve years. She had seen every doctor, tried every remedy. She knew only that if she could press through the crowds and even just touch Jesus's garment, she would be healed.

It was illegal for this woman to be out with the people. She was bleeding. She was unclean. It was against the law that she, a woman, would touch Jesus, a man. But against all the laws and against all the odds, she reached out to Jesus, she pressed into him with everything she had, and she was healed.

Jesus recognized this woman as one of his own. He called her "daughter."

Daughter, Jesus recognizes you as well. His face is turned toward you in kind intent. You can come to him with your whole story. Everything you are as a woman and everything you are not. You can bring him your victories and your failures and your fears. He will withhold no good thing from you. He will not turn his face away.

Jesus, I come to touch your robe today. Look at me. Hear me. See me. Heal me. In your name I pray, amen.

46

---

just believe

Don't be afraid; just believe.
—Mark 5:36

I love the story of Jairus and Jesus found in Mark 5. Jesus had just crossed over the lake, and Jairus—a leader in the synagogue—had gone down to meet him. Actually, he didn't just go down to meet him; he went down to fall at his feet. He asked Jesus—no, he pleaded with Jesus—to heal his daughter. And Jesus, being fully himself, said he would.

But on the way to Jairus's home, a servant came to meet Jairus and told him that his daughter had died. "Why bother the teacher anymore?" Jesus turned to Jairus and spoke the same words he is speaking to us today: "Don't be afraid; just believe."

In the face of the impossible, Jesus told Jairus (and tells us) to believe. With the words spoken that Jairus's worst fear had come true, Jesus said, "Don't give in to fear. You may not see the way, but with me nothing is impossible. I am good. You can trust me."

Jairus did not leave Jesus then. Jairus continued to press on with him to his home and invited Jesus to his dead daughter's bedside. Somewhere deep inside Jairus, a spark of hope had flared that even his deepest fear coming true could not quench.

And you know what happened next. Jesus said to the little girl, "Get up." So she did. Who could possibly resist the call of Jesus?

Hear Jesus saying these words to your spirit today: "Don't give into fear, my child. You may not see the way, but with me nothing is impossible. I am good. You can trust me. I am coming soon."

47

---

the final word

Praise the LORD, my soul;
all my inmost being, praise his holy name.
—Psalm 103:1

A few years ago on my morning walk and time with God, and after many years of praying for this, I felt the cement blocks of fear I have carried in my heart around the lives of my sons fall off. Just fall *off*. It was one of those instances when the veil between heaven and earth is so very thin. In those moments, I know the goodness of God, the surety of heaven, the power and authority of being Jesus's. In that particular moment, I believed the truth that I had absolutely nothing to fear on behalf of my boys or my husband. Or me. Nothing.

As soon as the weight came off, my thoughts surprised me. I felt a freedom to *want*. The desire to skydive reemerged. (Where had that gone?) The desire surfaced to ride bikes and climb mountains and have dinner parties and know Jesus like crazy and teach women and speak at arenas and *live my life*. Fully. With abandon.

What happens when God comes and releases us from long-held fears or fears that have long held us? What happens when we surrender fear to God and invite his love to overwhelm it? What is on the other side of fear? Is it faith? Yes, but the form it takes is desire.

When fears dissipate, desires surface that you didn't even know you had. Freedom rises to embrace your life and live it. I mean really live it. To live unabashedly. Desires rise in your heart for yourself and for others. Desires awaken regarding what you want to offer, do, experience, *become*. No longer bound by fear, how high can we soar? How deep can we dive? How much delight can we experience? Yes, there will be sorrow too—it's a part of the deal—but life gets the final word. *Life*. Life always gets the final word. Every single time. Forever.

Jesus, what do you want me to desire today? What dreams are waiting for me when I let go of fear? Show me the freedom you want me to embrace. Amen!

48

---

a heavenly exchange

A bruised reed he will not break,
and a smoldering wick he will not snuff out.
In faithfulness he will bring forth justice.
—Isaiah 42:3

Fear is not our ally. It is not our destiny. The things we fear are in the way of our coming closer to Jesus, receiving his love, and being perfected by his love. We want to allow God to reveal what fears we have that we may not even know we have, and then we want to respond by raising the white flag of surrender. Surrender. Not to the fear. But to God. To his love. To allow his perfect love to cast out fear and then to receive what he desires for us instead.

There is no shame here. The places where we still fear are simply the places we have yet to fully receive God's love. Only by his grace and in his love can we let go of our fear. Let go and *receive*. Receive his dreams.

Receive his love. It is an exchange of fear for desire. It is an exchange of death for life.

There is no fear in love. And I can tell you this with certainty: God does not want you to live in fear. And he does want you to live.

You probably know what you have been afraid to entrust to God. When we surrender our fear, we are offering it to Jesus. We are saying, "This fear is too much fear for me to bear. I give it to you because I believe you are good and worthy of my trust." When we actively, by faith, lay down our fears at the feet of Jesus, we pick up his love in return. It is an uneven trade. A heavenly exchange.

Jesus, my fear about [___] is too much for me to bear. I lay it at your feet. Let me receive your love, your peace, your joy in return. Amen.

saying yes to God's plan

And they have defeated him by the blood of the Lamb
and by their testimony.
And they did not love their lives so much
that they were afraid to die.
—Revelation 12:11 NLT

Several years ago John and I went through a particularly hard time. We faced a great deal of spiritual attack. At one point it was so severe that I thought John might lose his life. I was *afraid*.

One night John came into the living room and said, "We have got to take this weapon out of the Enemy's hand. He is using fear against us. Fear about me." We talked about the passage in Revelation 12 that says the saints overcome the Evil One by the blood of Jesus. They had no fear—especially about death.

John and I knelt down. We confessed our fears to Jesus. We gave him total control over our lives, including the timing of our deaths. We renounced fear, and we made peace with the fact that our lives are in God's hands. It was a turning point for us. The fear lost its brutal grip.

Laying down what we want to protect or are afraid of losing or are terrified we will never have is not the same thing as losing those things. It is *surrendering* them. It is opening up our clenched hand around them and allowing God access to them and to us. It is actually saying yes to God for them. Yes to his plan. Yes to his way. It is believing that just as his ways are higher than the heavens are above the earth, so his way for the things we fear is higher. This God of ours is a God of life, of goodness. He is the God of the Resurrection. We lay down our fear. We pick up Jesus. He is the only way we can live beyond fear. He is the Way.

Jesus, reveal to me what I am afraid of. What or whom am I not trusting you with? Just help me picture it, imagine it, see their faces. Lord, I want to trust you. Would you please help me give you my lingering fear? Come for me here, Jesus. Please help me. I need you. In your name, amen.

50

---

the power of friendships

As iron sharpens iron,
so one person sharpens another.
—Proverbs 27:17

No woman is meant to live her life as a solo act. We need other women to help us on our way. Supporting us. Encouraging us. Challenging us. Calling us to do what we are meant to do and become who we are meant to become.

Men do that for women, and women do that for men. But we women receive things from women that we do not receive from men. And no one knows what it's like to be a woman better than another woman.

A woman can be strong yet tender. Powerful yet soft. Fierce with the potential to be kind. Wise but sometimes foolish. Romantic. Cynical. Merciful. Wounded. Beautiful. Silly. Nurturing. Mysterious even to herself. Courageous. Odd. Vulnerable. Beaten down through the centuries yet continually rising up generation after generation. Feared and fearsome. Get a group of them together, moving toward the same goal, and power is released. Nations are forged. Justice is spread. The kingdom of God *advances*.

Though at times it may be tempting to resign ourselves to a circle of polite and superficial female relationships, it is not a wise thing. We need women with whom we can be honest about the realities of our lives, both the internal and the external realities. We need women friends who offer us truth in return. We need relationships with women in all their manifest forms, but mostly we need to have a few women *friends*.

God created us to be in relationship. He created us to sharpen and strengthen one another. So never discount the impact of women's friendships. They truly have the potential to change the world!

Jesus, I've tried to hide parts of me, even from myself. Will you look at them with me … and show me how you see me? Will you also bring others into my life who can help me see the truth about who I am and who you are?

51

forever friends

There are "friends" who destroy each other,
but a real friend sticks closer than a brother.
—Proverbs 18:24 NLT

I have a very dear friend who in her fierce loyalty to me signs many of her cards and emails with "Your forever friend." She writes that to me, fully aware that I am no longer certain such a thing exists on this side of eternity. My heart has become wary, and my friend pushes against my wariness in loving and unyielding proclamations of faithful friendship. In the face of her love, my heart is softening. In the face of her consistent offer of relationship, my heart is healing. Friends can wound at times, deeply, yes. But friends can bless too. Profoundly.

Friends are sometimes referred to as "Jesus with skin on," people sharing our humanity and reminding us that God loves us. We need to be reminded of that truth often. Left to ourselves, we quickly forget everything that is vital to remember. Companionship and friendship are human needs, as necessary to our becoming ourselves as air to our lungs and food to our bodies.

A good friend loves you when you are hilarious and when you are hurting. A true friend loves you when you are being kind and when you are PMS-ing all over the place. She may not love what you are doing, or the dragon you are manifesting, but she loves *you*. She knows who the true you is, and even in the midst of your living as an impostor to your very self, a friend calls you up and out. A friend sees who you are meant to be and beckons you to rise to the higher version of yourself.

Friendship is a high and holy thing. It's true that it can also be messy. Friendships with women are not for the faint of heart. But they are worth it.

Jesus, you are my only true "forever friend." I want to embrace that truth every day so that I might love and pursue my earthly friends with a free and giving heart! Amen.

52

satisfaction

*I no longer call you servants, because a servant
does not know his master's business. Instead, I have
called you friends, for everything that I learned
from my Father I have made known to you.*
—John 15:15

Friendship is meant to provide a refuge from loneliness, and a respite from self-criticism and the critique of a never-satisfied world. It is a place where our hearts don't have to work quite so hard to be heard and understood and accepted. Friendship is supposed to offer a taste of what is coming when our souls will be fully known and completely at rest.

But it is just a taste. I have found that the people I love and who love me deeply are not able to satisfy my insatiable soul in a lasting way. But man, have I wanted them to. "Fill me!" I've cried. "Satisfy me!" John has tried to fill me. Friends have tried to fill me. And their offerings have been marvelous. But never enough. I have a leak. Really, it's a break in the pipe. Aware of my own brokenness, I have tried to hide it and get other people to tend it. It hasn't worked. My demanding has backfired. I have learned the hard way—and just about everything I have learned, I have learned the hard way—the beautiful freeing truth that Jesus is the only one who can satisfy me. He's actually the only one who is meant to!

Coming to know Jesus more as my primary forever Friend is freeing my heart to offer and receive the amazing gift of friendship. Friendship, fellowship, is a gift, one that each of us is meant to enjoy and offer. We need each other. But in order to continue to move toward one another and receive freely what others are meant to share with us, we need Jesus.

God, you created the universe and yet you call me "friend." I want to know you more deeply as my best friend, the friend who always is there for me, always understands me, and always loves me completely.

perfect love

God blesses those who are merciful,
for they will be shown mercy.
—Matthew 5:7 NLT

Who among us has not suffered betrayal at the hands of a trusted friend? Who among us has not shrunk away in response to being hurt? Which one of us has not been responsible for wounding another? We all have.

We *all* have.

We need Jesus. We need mercy. We need healing. We are not meant to live this life alone, and we won't get very far along on our journey if we try. We don't have the luxury of insisting we will never be hurt again. We don't get to insist on anything, really. Except maybe we can insist on continuing to press in to Jesus, no matter what.

He's here. He's waiting. He has never betrayed you, and he never will. He is the Source of our true

identity. He is the One we must look to first to fill us
with truth, acceptance, and love. Then we can bring
our hearts, be they bursting with joy or battered by
life, to our friends without demanding that they fill
us. We can offer ourselves, open to receive good gifts
from them but vigilant to stay close to our God and
screening every experience, every word, through him.
He has promised to never leave you or forsake you. He
is the same yesterday, today, and forever. He is perfect
love, and he loves you perfectly. And he's not going
anywhere.

*Jesus, I give to you now my memories of hurtful words
spoken to me, times when I was betrayed, times when I
was ignored or neglected as a friend. I also give to you now
the times when I was the one who spoke hurtful words,
who betrayed, ignored, or neglected others. Redeem my
friendships. We need your mercy. Amen.*

54

surrendering

For everything there is a season, and a
time for every matter under heaven.
—Ecclesiastes 3:1 ESV

It was a revelation to me to realize that not every friend in our lives is meant to walk with us through the remainder of our lives. Friendships do change. People change. You change. You are supposed to.

Several years ago I realized I was holding a particular friendship with a clenched fist rather than a loose hand. We had been friends for many years, and I assumed we would be friends for the rest of our lives. I ignored the telltale signs of change. This friend had been moving away from me for quite a long while, but I absolutely refused to see it. I wanted what *I* wanted. I thought she was fabulous. Surely she had to feel the same way about me!

Somewhere along the way, my desire for relationship turned into demand, and demand is one of the death knells of a friendship. I needed to unclench my fist and in love let my friend go. I also needed to invite Jesus into the places of my heart that had refused to see that it was time to let her go.

Insisting. Demanding. Refusing. These are not actions that lead to the life Jesus has for us.

Releasing. Surrendering. Embracing freedom. These are the actions Jesus calls us to. These are the signs of a loving friendship—a friendship that sometimes needs to let go.

Are there any relationships in your life right now that you need to hold with more open hands?

our biggest cheerleaders

Whoever walks with the wise becomes wise.
—Proverbs 13:20 ESV

Many people, including women, underestimate the closeness of heart that women friends are capable of reaching. It can be excruciating to let a friend go or, worse, to be let go of.

How well I remember sobbing in the arms of a precious friend when my young family was moving across the country. It felt as if my heart were being torn out.

How difficult it is when a friendship ends because of offenses, misunderstandings, anger, or betrayal. How searingly painful it is when God calls you to walk away from a cherished friend when love and unity have left the relationship.

Sometimes a friendship ends simply because your paths no longer cross. Churches split. Bible studies end. Children switch schools. Gyms close. People move. Jobs change. The natural and easy ways that we as friends connect shift under our feet, and it takes enormous effort on *both* sides for the friendship to shift and continue as well. Perhaps it is meant to continue. Perhaps it isn't. Some friends we are called to fight for and some we are called to release.

We are meant to grow and change and become throughout the duration of our lives, and we need to be surrounded by people who celebrate the person we are *becoming*. Our true friends are people who are our biggest cheerleaders and encourage us on to the next higher version of ourselves that God is calling us to.

Thank you, God, for people who encourage me to be faithful to you.

56

jealousy and envy

A heart at peace gives life to the body,
but envy rots the bones.
—Proverbs 14:30

Walking with a friend through trials requires much tenderness, grace, and wisdom on our part, but it is actually more difficult to walk with a friend through a season of success and blessing. "We didn't get a vacation like that." "I wish I had been given the opportunity to travel." "I love their new sofa. I wish I had a new sofa." Careful.

Jealousy and envy are two death knells to a friendship. God does not want us to be jealous of what our friends receive or achieve. We are called to rejoice with them. We want only the best for our friends always.

I know that's a challenge—it certainly is in my own life. Loving people through travail and success requires much from us. God is always at work sifting and shaping, purifying and clarifying what is in our hearts. To stay in relationship with another person requires first that we stay in relationship with God. He is the only way we can navigate through jealousies that rear their ugly heads or offenses from others that prick our vulnerable hearts.

The truth is, a good part of our becoming takes place in the sanctifying work of relationships. And not because friendship is always a greenhouse either. Trees grow strong because of winds; drought forces their roots to go deeper. There isn't anything on earth like relationships to make you holy. When our frail humanity is revealed in some way we and others don't like, we bring it to God. We ask for forgiveness. We ask for his life to fill us and his love to flow through us, which means "Christ in me, love through me" becomes a regular prayer. It always comes back to Jesus.

Jesus, this is tough for me … I want to choose friends wisely, and I want to stick with those friendships and grow through any hard times. Will you please help me be the kind of friend you want me to be? In Jesus's name, amen.

57

---

bff?

Be devoted to one another in love. Honor
one another above yourselves.
—Romans 12:10

For many years I thought that a cherished best, *best* friend would be a woman who understood me at all times and enjoyed *all* the same things I enjoyed. She'd want to go to a movie when I wanted to go to a movie, and she would want to see the same show I wanted to see. She would be passionately in love with Jesus and desire him above all else, and she would always point my heart back to him. I would do the same for her, and she would think I was amazing and wise and justified in my mood swings. She would be available to me whenever I called and would be encouraging and empathetic. She would vote for the same candidates I vote for. She would always get my jokes and want to eat at the same restaurant I wanted to eat at, and she would never be offended by a failure of mine.

Embarrassing, right?

The truth is, I have more than my share of amazing friends. And I am learning that each of these variously gifted women offers something of unique value that the others don't. Their very differences from each other and from me enrich my life! God is meeting my need for friendship, just not through one woman. Some women are blessed with a best friend, but most women aren't. Most of us have a few friends who provide something we need, and we provide something they need. Our hearts are met in many ways, by the beautiful offerings of a few. I don't think a human being is actually able to bear the burden of being someone's one and only. God alone can be our One and Only.

God understands us all the time. He is available every moment. People don't and aren't. They have lives and schedules and a myriad of people pulling on them, and that makes them normal and not at our beck and call. Jesus calls us "friend." Oh, to know him more deeply as that. I want to know him as my King and my God and my Friend who enjoys me fully, accepts me completely, and loves me unconditionally. Because that is who he is.

Dear Jesus, you never leave me or forsake me. You understand me and everything I am going through. You want to spend time with me. Please help me press into knowing you as my closest friend. I need you. I'd love to have close women friends too, so would you please bring them to me? And help me be a good friend as well? Thank you, Lord. I love you. In your name I pray.

58

honestly

We will speak the truth in love, growing in
every way more and more like Christ.
—Ephesians 4:15 NLT

Scripture exhorts us to speak the truth *in love*, which
means we shouldn't speak the truth in anger or resentment or with the desire to wound. We need to be
careful to check our underlying motives for speaking
the truth. We should be aware of the reason behind
our desire to share something. We want to know that
we are speaking the truth with the desire to love and
to bless.

The Bible does *not* exhort us to speak everything
that is true. In our culture of honesty, we may feel com-
pelled to share everything with our husband or with
our close friends, even the negative things. We want to
be honest, right? We don't want to have secrets from
each other, right? Wrong. Sharing every thought or

emotion that goes through your head will wreak havoc on the relationship.

No friendship, no marriage, has the capacity to carry the burdens of our every nuance. Only Jesus does. He knows us. We don't shock him. We are not too much for him. Sharing truth with a friend or a husband in the desire to keep nothing between us can overwhelm the person and the relationship. No relationship, a friendship or a marriage, can sustain the brunt of total honesty. Relationships are not meant to be the dumping grounds of every negative thought, belief, or emotion.

Dear one, they don't need to know everything. When we are struggling with negative emotions, we bring them to Jesus and maybe to a counselor, a pastor, our spouse, or a different trustworthy friend. And when we are through with the negative, separating feelings, we don't dredge them back up and pour them out onto the heart of the one we have finally come to terms with. We can do great damage to one another in the name of honesty.

As women growing into the fullness of who we are created to be, we speak only the truth that God calls us to speak, in love, and only when he calls us to speak it.

Jesus, you are my best friend. You are someone I can be completely honest with, someone who loves me completely. What can you and I do together today to enjoy our friendship? I really want to hear you!

59

———

let it go

[Love] keeps no record of wrongs.
—1 Corinthians 13:5

Too often we keep lists of wrongs done to us in marriage or friendship. We say we forgive—and we may even believe we have—but when offenses come up again, we notice them with a sort of sick satisfaction: "See what I mean?"

The word used in Scripture for *offense* actually means "bait," like the bait that is placed inside a trap to lure an animal to its death. When we dwell on our hurts, we have taken the bait of offense. We are inside the trap.

Unless offenses are forgiven, they will poison the relationship. The poison seeps out and affects our own souls as well. Offenses we hold on to lead to death.

Jesus took all our offenses into his broken body when he died for us, and he took everyone else's as well.

All that he suffered—the beating, the scourging, the mocking, and finally the crucifixion—was more than enough to pay for it all; our offenses and theirs.

Once when I was reeling from being badly hurt by a person, something wicked rose up in me and I had to admit that, ugly as it was, I wanted that person to suffer for it as much as I was suffering. A picture immediately came to my mind of Jesus, tortured and bleeding. The Holy Spirit asked, "Is this suffering enough?" Yes. Yes, it is. Sometimes in our humanity we may feel that in order for justice to be done, people need to pay for their offenses. Well, Jesus took their bill. It's been paid for.

With the help of God, we must choose to forgive. Let it go. Let them go. Come out of the trap.

Dear God, I forgive all those who have hurt me, and I bless them in Jesus's name. I pray only more of you to them, for them. And I forgive myself for having hurt others. Please fill me with your Spirit and live and love through me that I might become a woman after your heart who loves others well. In Jesus's name, amen.

crucified to the world

*May I never boast except in the cross of our
Lord Jesus Christ, through which the world has
been crucified to me, and I to the world.*
—Galatians 6:14

The cross changes every relationship. Even family ties.
Jesus tells us, "Anyone who loves their father or mother
more than me is not worthy of me; anyone who loves
their son or daughter more than me is not worthy of
me. Whoever does not take up their cross and follow
me is not worthy of me" (Matt. 10:37–38).

All ties are subject now to the rule of Christ. And
so we can say, in a very godly and healthy way, "I am
crucified to the world, and the world is crucified to me.
I am crucified to my mom, to my sister, to my friend,
and to my enemy, and they are crucified to me."

The only bond Scripture urges us to maintain is
the bond of love by the Holy Spirit. All others—well,

it's time to break them. You won't believe how free you can be and how good you can feel!

It is very important to note that breaking a soul tie with a person is not the same thing as *rejecting* the person. It is actually the *loving* thing to do. You don't want the person obsessing about you, and you don't want to be obsessing about her. You don't want her controlling you, and you don't want to be controlling her. You certainly don't want her warfare, and she doesn't want yours.

This simple prayer that follows will help you break unholy bonds.

By the cross of Jesus Christ, I now sever all soul ties with _____ in the name of Jesus Christ. I am crucified to her, and she is crucified to me. I bring the cross of Christ between us, and I bring the love of Christ between us. I send _____'s spirit back to her body, and I forbid her warfare to transfer to me or to my domain. I command my spirit back into the Spirit of Jesus Christ in my body. I release _____ to you, Jesus. I entrust her to you. Bless her, God! In Jesus's name, amen.

61

treasures

*Every good and perfect gift is from above, coming
down from the Father of the heavenly lights,
who does not change like shifting shadows.*
—James 1:17

I have prayed to have friends. I have sought them out
and pursued them. At times I have been desperate for
them. But the best ones have come to me as a surprise,
unexpected answers to prayers I had forgotten I'd
prayed. Friends are gifts to us straight from the heart of
God to our own, and no one is better at giving perfect
gifts than he is.

They come to us in all sorts of ways, these treasures. One I met while our children played at a park
and I helped her dig through the sand to find her son's
precious lost toy. One sat next to me at church one
morning, both of us holding our infant sons, reluctant
to relinquish them to the nursery. One came to me

through an introduction at a party followed by a shy invitation to meet over coffee.

How happy I was the other day to listen to a voice message from a dear one who didn't speak but merely sang to me, "I just called to say I love you …" At the sound of her voice, joyful and whimsical, encouragement lightened my weighed-down heart.

Women friends are gems to be treasured and asked for. They lend each other their clothes, their recipes, their courage, their ideas, their faith, and their hope. Oh, to be loved and seen and encouraged to continue to sing one's song, to offer one's true heart!

The deepest desire of every human being's heart is to be loved. To be loved in the face of our flaws and failings is a taste of heaven. In heaven we will be completely transformed into the image of Christ, beholding him as he truly is, and we will finally and fully be who we truly are. God knows us inside and out. Right now. In heaven we will know him. And we will know others and be known by them perfectly as well. Not only known but enjoyed. Embraced. Understood. Celebrated. Loved. What a thought. And what an extraordinary gift it is on this side of paradise to be known and enjoyed here. That's what friendship is for.

Thank you, God, for friendship. You knew that we would need significant relationships to help us know you more. You knew that I would need other women in my life. Thank you for loving me in this way!

62

the window of grace

The joy of the LORD is your strength.
—Nehemiah 8:10

I was busy inside and out, driving to and fro on a stream of errands. I was tired and not happy about it. I called my friend Rosetta in the middle of my lists to say hello but also to complain a little. She didn't let me. Not even a little bit. Instead, she spoke words of loving conviction: "How wonderful that you can get out! How great that you have such a full life! Oh, to be able to walk!" Rosetta's life wasn't full with running errands or with running of any kind. She couldn't run. She couldn't walk. Living in a wheelchair, Rose didn't get out much. But she had so much life exuding out of her spirit that sometimes, to my embarrassment, I would forget.

Her words, the words of a friend who knew and loved me, reframed my moment and opened my eyes. Friends do that for one another.

Rosetta spent many of her days looking out the window in her tiny apartment, watching the activity of others more physically able. Her little view of the world was a window of grace, and she invited me to see my life through it. In her company my priorities ordered themselves up correctly. She taught me that love sees with a thankful heart. The simple moments that I, too, often take for granted are the very pearls that join together and make a beautiful life, but only when strung together with thankfulness, linked with grace, shared with an open hand.

Rosetta is running now. She is free and healed and happy and seeing face-to-face the One who has won her heart. I will always miss her, though I know I will see her in just a little while. For now, I pray I continue to see my life through a window of grace and, in loving friendships, invite others to share the view.

God, it's amazing what you teach me through the words and lives of other women. I want to receive those truths. I want to live with open hands of grace as well.

floodwaters

In this world you will have trouble.
—John 16:33

The Yampa River flooded its banks in western Colorado in 2011. In Steamboat Springs, Colorado, it flooded both parks and parking lots. It encroached upon people's lawns and homes. Residents stacked sandbags against it. Still it rushed on, brown and churning. It would subside. But not for a while yet. Not until the snowpack finished melting.

The river will have its way. The snowpack that winter had rivers flooding all over the western states, and in addition to flooding, the result was an abundance of wildflowers beyond reckoning. They were *gorgeous.* Purple larkspur and yellow arrowleaf carpeted the hillsides. A plethora of flowers—red, purple, blue, white, yellow—painted the world with breathtaking beauty.

The price of which was paid in sandbags.

In the midst of suffering, it can feel impossible to see the beauty beyond it. Yes, spring only arrives after winter. Tulips will bloom only if they have endured a freeze. Beauty does come from ashes. But it takes intention to believe these things when all we see is pain.

Over thousands of years, water carved the Grand Canyon—one of the most beautiful displays of nature in the world. My face too is being etched. My soul is being carved. Forces are at work sculpting me—my life, my views, and my beliefs—honing and shaping and changing me. The process is sometimes painful, but the effect? Oh, for the grace to see the effect as beautiful. To be able to see our lives, our bodies, our faces, our souls sculpted by time, our choices, and the hand of our relentless, fierce, and loving God as beautiful displays.

Rain serves a purpose. Even floodwaters. Even suffering.

Jesus, I call to you and you save me. You rescue me from the floods, from the rising waters. You bring life and color and beauty out of my suffering. I praise you for bringing purpose out of pain! Amen.

64

true victory

*Dear friends, do not be surprised at the fiery
ordeal that has come on you to test you, as though
something strange were happening to you.*
—1 Peter 4:12

Peter tells us not to let pain surprise us. But we are
surprised, aren't we? We wonder what we did wrong
or if we're wrong about God. What we believe about
God is quickly exposed by pain. What's he like, *really*?
Is he mean? Is he harsh? Is he mad at us? Does he not
care? Does he not see? Did we fall through the cracks
of the universe?

I went to get a mammogram with one of my
girlfriends. She suggested we go together so that we
actually *would* go, and then we could celebrate having
it over with by going out to lunch. We did. A week later
when I next saw her, I asked, "Did you get your clean-
bill-of-health letter?" She didn't get that letter. She got

a phone call. And another mammogram. And a biopsy. And the battle for her life. I came out as normal, and she came out with stage IV breast cancer. It felt like our two names had been put in a hat, and this time her name was drawn.

The first thing painful trials try to do is separate us from God. But being separated from God is the worst thing that can happen, much worse than the trial itself.

How do you understand your life? Why has it turned out so differently from what you imagined? What do you make of its randomness?

I certainly haven't figured out the answers to all those questions. I do know that Christianity is not a promise to enjoy a life without pain, nor is it a shortcut through it. It is a promise that pain, sorrow, sin—ours and others'—will not swallow us, destroy us, define us, or have the final word. Jesus has won the victory. And in him so have we.

Dear Jesus, help me to believe you today and to put my trust in your victory rather than my ability to take a detour around pain. I can't. But even in pain, I confess that you are more than enough for me. In your name I pray.

far from eden

*When tempted, no one should say, "God is tempting
me." For God cannot be tempted by evil, nor does he
tempt anyone; but each person is tempted when they
are dragged away by their own evil desire and enticed.
Then, after desire has conceived, it gives birth to sin;
and sin, when it is full-grown, gives birth to death.*
—James 1:13–15

A terrible flu swept through our area recently. It hit
us hard, but it hit a friend of mine harder. As I talked
with her one day, she confessed, "I wish I would learn
what God is trying to teach me so I could get over
this flu."

What was she assuming about God? She was
assuming that sickness was from him. That simply isn't
true. Our current address is far from Eden. We live in
a fallen world with broken people, and we ourselves
are not yet all we are meant to be. The flu goes around.

Sickness is not a punishment from God. He is not waiting for my friend to grasp some deeper truth about herself or to repent of some hidden sin before he heals her. He is not holding out on her to finally get her act together in order to bless her. He is not a mean God but a loving one filled with grace and mercy. It is his kindness that draws us to repentance, not his cruelty. God will use painful trials, even the flu, to hone us, but he doesn't cause them.

Some of you have been taught a theology that God causes all things. So you have to swallow hard and believe that God caused you to be sexually abused, God caused your mother to die young, God caused your child to abandon the faith.

Oh, friends, this is a horrible view of God and a profound *heresy*. James makes it clear that God does not tempt anyone to sin. But people are tempted every day. So, then, things happen every single day that God is *not* causing. God does not make anyone sin, but people sin every day, *and those sins have terrible consequences.* This is not God doing these things. Do you see what an important difference this makes in our understanding of God's thoughts toward us?

Jesus, I am struggling today. I know you have not caused the pain I am in, but I ask you to be with me here in this pain. Help me see what it can teach me about your love for me and your calling on my life. In Jesus's name.

66

the doorway of suffering

In all their distress he too was distressed.
—Isaiah 63:9

Ever since Adam and Eve sinned, this world has been badly, badly broken. Although God did not cause the brokenness, he can use our suffering to shape us. We need to ask Jesus for his interpretation of what we are experiencing. Our interpretation of the events will shape everything that follows. It will shape our emotions, our perspective, and our decisions.

I've learned that when it comes to suffering, you can have understanding or you can have Jesus. If you insist on understanding, you usually lose both.

When suffering enters into your life, the first thing to do is to invite Jesus into it. Pray, *Jesus, catch my heart*. When painful trials come your way, by all means ask God what's up—ask him to interpret it for you. But whether he provides understanding or not,

invite Jesus in. Keep inviting Jesus into the pain. Invite
Jesus into the places in your heart that are rising to the
surface through the suffering, whether they be painful
memories, unbelief, or self-contempt. Pray, *Please come
meet me here, Jesus. I need you.*

Suffering may be the door you walk through that
draws you to deeper intimacy with Jesus. Suffering can
do that, if we let it. And though it would never be the
doorway we would choose, it is one we will never regret
walking through.

What is a situation for which you need to pray, *Jesus,
catch my heart?*

67

---

acquainted with grief

Never will I leave you;
never will I forsake you.
—Hebrews 13:5

Let suffering play its sanctifying role. God does work all things for our good. He will use pain to expose our false beliefs about our hearts and about his heart. He will use it to prick a place in us that has been wounded here before, to reveal our brokenness so that he can heal it. He will use suffering to reveal Jesus's faithfulness, kindness, and unending love for us.

You see, there is more going on here than meets the eye. There is a battle raging over the human heart. Will we love God and choose to trust the goodness of his heart in the face of the immense brokenness of the world? Will we stand in our belief that God is worthy of our worship and praise in the face of the immense brokenness in our world?

We can know that in our distress, God too is distressed. Jesus understands heartbreak, betrayal, abandonment, loneliness, sorrow, and pain. He is acquainted with grief. He cares. He cares for you.

In Hebrews 13, God promises that he will never leave us or forsake us. The original Greek is difficult to translate because of the strong emphasis on *never*—it's a triple negative. God wants you to know that you will never, never, never be abandoned by him. Ever. Never ever. He promises to never leave you or forsake you no matter what you've done or what you are suffering. We hold on to that.

God will never *leave me or forsake me. Never, never, never. I hold on to this promise today.*

beauty from ashes

The Spirit of the Sovereign LORD is on me,
because the LORD has anointed me
to proclaim good news to the poor.
He has sent me to bind up the brokenhearted,
to proclaim freedom for the captives
and release from darkness for the prisoners,
to proclaim the year of the LORD's favor
and the day of vengeance of our God,
to comfort all who mourn,
and provide for those who grieve in Zion—
to bestow on them a crown of beauty
instead of ashes,
the oil of joy
instead of mourning,
and a garment of praise
instead of a spirit of despair.
They will be called oaks of righteousness,

a planting of the LORD
for the display of his splendor.
—Isaiah 61:1–3

There may not be a more beautiful passage in all of Scripture than Isaiah 61. *This* is where Jesus declared what he came to do. He came to heal the brokenhearted, to set the captive free. He came to restore us in him and to him. He came to comfort those who grieve, to bestow on them a crown of beauty instead of ashes and a garment of praise instead of a spirit of despair. He says that sorrow may last for the night, but joy comes in the morning. It comes with the morning star. It comes with Jesus. Always.

Jesus, heal my broken heart, release me from all darkness. Comfort me in my suffering. Cleanse me from all evil that has gotten in or taken root in the places of my sorrow. Give me a crown of beauty instead of ashes. Make me beautiful here, Lord, in this. Lift my grief and sorrow and give me the oil of your gladness instead of mourning. Give me a garment of praise instead of a spirit of despair.

69

finding peace

My heart has heard you say, "Come and talk with me."
And my heart responds, "LORD, I am coming."
—Psalm 27:8 NLT

Remember the old bumper sticker "Jesus Is the Answer"? I used to mock that bumper sticker. *What's the question?* I'd think. "How long do you bake a potato?" "Jesus." "Where should I get my car insurance from?" "Jesus." But the older I get, the surer I become that the bumper sticker had it right. Jesus *is* the answer. He is the answer to every substantive question of my heart and need in my soul. And boy, do my needs and questions surface when I am distressed.

How do you find peace in the midst of difficult, painful circumstances? Let Peace find you. He's right where you are, right smack-dab in the middle of your life.

In the midst of our joy, our busyness, our sorrow, and our suffering, we must turn our gaze on

Jesus. Invite Jesus in. Ask him to prove to you once again that he is who he says he is. He says he is our Strength. Our Shield. Our Rock. Our Hiding Place. Our Refuge. Our Deliverer. Our great Comforter, our faithful Companion, and our ever-present Friend. Jesus says he is the mighty God, the Prince of Peace. We can trust him.

Jesus is the only one who can meet the deepest needs of your heart, and he wants you to know that he loves you so much that he's moved heaven and earth to do it. He is the only one who will never disappoint you, never ever leave you, comfort you intimately, and love you perfectly every single moment of your life. Invite him in. He *is* the Answer.

Jesus, I praise you today because you are my Deliverer. My Rock. My Shield. My Hiding Place. My Comforter. My best Friend. My Strength and my Refuge. You are the mighty God, the Prince of Peace, and I trust you!

70

---

leaning into God

Thank God no matter what happens.
—1 Thessalonians 5:18 MSG

My mother was a very driven woman. She could be controlling and demanding. She failed in many ways. Not in every way, not by a long shot, but she did have her rough edges.

My mother also loved Jesus. When cancer began to ravage her life when she was seventy-one, a startling transformation began to take place. My mother softened. She became gentler. She loosened her grasp on control. She lost her edge to demand or criticize. She said "I love you" more than she ever had. The beauty that was always there began to come forth in truly amazing ways. Our last four months together were the best months of love and relationship we ever shared.

My mother suffered intensely during the last months of her life. But in those final months, she leaned into God and came to know his love in a way that filled her heart with peace and joy. During that time, my mom was unable to swallow anything, so she received nourishment via a feeding tube. She hoped that when she crossed over from life to Life, Jesus would be waiting for her with a large, cold glass of water.

A few months after my mom died, I came across a note in her precious handwriting. This is what it said: "I had an unexpected diagnosis, and it has been the most awesome, rewarding, and glorious time God has ever given to me. I thank God the Father, Son, and Holy Spirit from the depth of my soul."

My mother actually gave thanks in her suffering— not *for* the suffering but for what it did in her life. It opened her up to relationship. It enabled her to offer love and receive love. And though her battle with cancer ended up costing my mom her life, what she gained through the pain she considered "the most awesome, rewarding, and glorious time God has ever given me."

And she's drinking Living Water now!

Jesus, I want to give thanks in my suffering today. Thanks for being in my suffering with me! May the pain I experience cause me to offer and receive love more abundantly. Amen.

71

the work of suffering

*So we're not giving up. How could we! Even though
on the outside it often looks like things are falling
apart on us, on the inside, where God is making new
life, not a day goes by without his unfolding grace.*
—2 Corinthians 4:16–17 MSG

Our friend Scott sent us a little note on the twenty-eighth anniversary of his fall from a ladder that left him paralyzed from the waist down. Scott and his wife know God in a way few of us do. He simply wrote, "No regrets." The note brought John and me to tears.

God didn't give my mom cancer any more than he caused Scott to fall. He didn't cause it. But he will use it. He will use it to reveal to us who he really is in the face of tragedy and anguish. He will use it to reveal to us who we really are. Jesus wants you to know who you are. He wants us to see ourselves as our Father sees us. The most important mirror for us to look in is our reflection in his eyes.

I would like to become a woman who is as desperate for God in my joy as I am in my sorrow. That has not happened yet. Nothing brings my heart to fully run after God like being in a season of grief. It may be grief over the way I have failed my sons or my husband. It may be sorrow over a revelation of how my selfishness has hurt my friends. It may be pain over the suffering that one whom I love is experiencing. But nothing causes me to seek God like pain.

Our dear friend's brother, Lance, just went to heaven. He was thirty years old and had spent the last eighteen months of his life in a courageous battle against brain cancer. Days before he died, his grieving mother wrote this: "If we don't let pain transform us, we will surely transmit it.… May all of our sorrow and loss be turned into compassion." Our loving God uses the pain and sorrow in our lives to transform us. Let it do its powerful sanctifying work.

Dear God, whether I experience joy or pain today, may it draw me closer to you.

72

giving thanks

*Rejoice always, pray continually, give
thanks in all circumstances.*
—1 Thessalonians 5:16–18

How do we allow suffering to do a holy work in us and
not let it make us envious, hard, angry women?

We need to be honest about what we *have* done
with our suffering. Have we become more fearful?
Controlling? Has resentment toward God or others
entered in? Let us quickly bring that to Jesus, for this
is cancer of the soul, and it ravages what God means
to make lovely. Let us renounce our anger or envy, our
controlling or bitterness. Let us ask God to remove
these things from our heart and soul.

Nothing—nothing—undoes the harmful effects
of suffering as our choice to worship Jesus in the midst
of it. That doesn't mean we must give thanks to God
for every wicked, evil, hard, painful, excruciating,

grief-filled thing that happens in our lives. That would be calling evil "good." No, my sister, what the scripture says is to give thanks to God *in* every situation, not *for* every situation.

By loving Jesus in our pain, we allow him *into* our pain. Being thankful opens up windows in the spiritual realm for the presence of God to fill our lives, our thoughts, our understanding, and our perspective. It opens up doors to the blessings God wants to pour into our lives. We will come to a place of increasing gratefulness for the story of our lives, both the joyful times and the excruciating seasons. We are on our way to the place of being able to exalt God over all of it. Yes, all of it.

Father God, use the pain in my life today to reveal your faithfulness, kindness, and love for me! Amen.

73

---

beautiful scars

*Put your finger here; see my hands. Reach out your hand
and put it into my side. Stop doubting and believe.*
—John 20:27

When Jesus rose from the dead and appeared to his disciples, Thomas was not present. So Jesus came back to
them again, when Thomas was also in their midst. Do
you recall how Jesus proved he was real, risen, and still
the same Jesus they had always known and loved? He
told Thomas, "Put your hands in my scars." Jesus still
had his scars then, and he still has them today. They are
Jesus's glory. They are what we most worship him for.
Glorified Jesus still has his scars, and when we reach
glory, so will we. But they will be beautiful, like his.

The story of my life and the struggles I have lived
with—and continue to live with—have helped shape me
into the woman I am today and the woman I am becoming. My scars, my struggles, my failures, my joys, my

private lonely agonies have been forging my soul into something beautiful. Eternal. Good. Yours have too.

Now we can fight that process—or we can yield to it. We can choose to let suffering soften us or harden us. We can choose whether we will allow it to make us more compassionate or let our hearts become jealous of others. We can choose whether we will love Jesus in it or resent him for it. Only one set of choices will make us more beautiful.

The pain we experience, the sorrow and the agony, serve a purpose. God *is* working all things together for our good. He is etching a masterpiece of stunning design. The beauty being forged in us through the transforming work of suffering is one that will leave us breathless, stunned, and forever thankful. And the crowning glory will be that because of the pain we have endured, we have come to know Jesus in a way that causes us to treasure the trial as one of God's greatest gifts to us. Amazing.

I choose today to let my suffering soften me to God's love. I choose to let my suffering make me more compassionate toward others. I choose to let my suffering make me more beautiful.

74

---

shake off your dust

Shake off your dust;
rise up, sit enthroned, Jerusalem.
Free yourself from the chains on your neck,
Daughter Zion, now a captive.
—Isaiah 52:2

John and I went to the zoo recently. We saw an amazing selection of birds—flamingos, California condors, and two bald eagles—enclosed in a habitat with high nets.

Later that day we went for a hike in the hills. We stopped at the cry of a hawk and looked up to see three of them soaring, diving so fast, then up, up, up. Chasing each other, then hovering and still—they flew with the aerial gymnastics of angels. They were awesome. They were *free*.

I felt bad for the birds I had just seen in captivity. At the zoo it had been wonderful to see bald eagles up close. How huge they are! But I've seen bald eagles eating fish on the banks of the Snake River. I've seen them looking out over their domain from the protected heights of a stately pine, and I've seen them battling golden eagles over their nests.

Freedom is better than captivity. So why does anyone choose captivity? Why do we live so long in the bondage we find ourselves in—the bondage of peer pressure, negative thoughts about ourselves, and fear?

I'd like every woman to hear Isaiah 52: "Free yourself from the chains on your neck." *Free yourself?* Isn't it Jesus who sets us free? Indeed he does. But we have a part to play in our freedom. God calls us to rise up, shake the dust off, sit enthroned.

After a while those animals in the zoo forget they were made for the open skies, the wild savannas. We don't want that to happen to us. We want to remember that God calls us to choose his grace, his truth, and our identity in him.

What is one thing you would like to be free of today? Sorrow? Regret? Self-contempt, shame, worry, doubts, addiction? In what ways does that struggle keep you in captivity?

Lord, show me how to free myself from this. I don't want to be held captive anymore!

75

---

where freedom begins

*Because I preach this Good News, I am suffering
and have been chained like a criminal. But
the word of God cannot be chained.*
—2 Timothy 2:9 NLT

Many years ago John and I were members of a wonderful church in Southern California. A young man also attended there who had an amazing spirit and an even more amazing testimony. "Daniel" was from Uganda. He had lived there under the brutal reign of Idi Amin. He had been in prison there, beaten, and tortured because he was a Christian—and he had the scars to show for it.

During one of Daniel's trials, he was hung from his feet and beaten over a period of days. The guard's job—his *job*—was to whip Daniel. After several days of this ritual torture, Daniel said to the guard as the guard was leaving, "Have a nice evening." A blessing.

By the grace of Jesus Christ living in his heart, Daniel was able to forgive his oppressors, and in that forgiveness he rose above the bondage they wanted over his life—the bondage of his heart, mind, and spirit.

"Have a nice evening."

The guard asked, "How can you say that to me?" Daniel told him how. He told him about the price Jesus had paid to win his heart, about the freedom he knew in Christ. He told him about being forgiven and accepted and loved perfectly.

A few days later, that guard helped Daniel escape. But first he took him home to feed him and have him share the gospel with his family.

Sometimes we assume that our circumstances must change and *then* we can experience freedom. Not so. God usually begins first with the transformation of our heart. Then he can change our circumstances.

Freedom begins with the choice to let Christ so invade our hearts that we choose to love, to forgive. We have been given the greatest freedom of all: freedom of heart, freedom from sin, a freedom that enables us to live and love as Jesus did.

Is there a circumstance that you have been hoping would change in your life? What would it look like to experience freedom *now*, even though the circumstance is the same?

no longer captives

Don't copy the behavior and customs of this world, but
let God transform you into a new person by changing
the way you think. Then you will learn to know God's
will for you, which is good and pleasing and perfect.
—Romans 12:2 NLT

How often have you heard, or thought, words like these?

"She talks too much and laughs too loud."
"She's too quiet."
"I can't believe she sends her kids to public school."
"I can't believe she homeschools her kids."
"She's going back to work; how awful."
"She doesn't work; she just stays home all day."

Women can be vicious. We cut with our words and even with a look. We bring others down as a way of building ourselves up. If we are insecure in ourselves or in our life choices, then people who make choices different from ours can feel threatening. We judge.

Judgments are dangerous. They are like curses. They release the hatred of the Enemy upon those we have judged.

God says to bless those who are cursing us. In his wild, free, and amazing love, he instructs us to pray blessing over people—pray blessing over people who have hurt you, judged you, maligned you, rejected you, or simply misunderstood you. Pray blessing on them. Pray more of Jesus for people! Because when they become blessed and happy and close to Jesus, they won't be judging you either!

We are no longer captives to sin. We are no longer slaves to the Enemy, to the world, or to our own flesh. We have been released. We are free to be transformed into the very image of Christ. We are free to love in the face of hatred. Free to become the fullest expression of our unique selves. Free to offer to others the beauty that God planted in us when he first dreamed of us.

Father, I don't need to judge other people for making different choices than I have. I don't need to cut other women down with my words or expressions. Forgive me. Show me how to love them, no matter what. In Jesus's name, amen.

77

---

free to fail

*It wasn't so long ago that you were mired in that old
stagnant life of sin. You let the world, which doesn't know
the first thing about living, tell you how to live. You filled
your lungs with polluted unbelief, and then exhaled
disobedience. We all did it, all of us doing what we felt like
doing, when we felt like doing it, all of us in the same boat.
It's a wonder God didn't lose his temper and do away with
the whole lot of us. Instead, immense in mercy and with an
incredible love, he embraced us. He took our sin-dead lives
and made us alive in Christ. He did all this on his own,
with no help from us! Then he picked us up and set us down
in highest heaven in company with Jesus, our Messiah.*
—Ephesians 2:1–6 MSG

Did you know you are free to fail today? Because of
Jesus, you can be free from the cages of other people's
expectations, demands, yokes, and judgments—including your own.

Perfectionism is a terrible prison. You don't need to live there.

Satan's goal is to keep you from living in the freedom that Jesus has purchased for you. Satan whispers to you when you have failed or sinned or are feeling horrid that you are nothing and no one. He is a liar. And your fight for your freedom involves exposing him for who he is even when the lies feel completely true. The battle is waged and won in your thought life: in your mind and in your heart.

You live under grace, not under judgment. You are loved, forgiven, embraced. Your emotions may waver. Your physical strength and spiritual life have variables. One day you are strong in Christ, believing everything God says, and another day you feel weak, doubtful, questioning.

That's okay. You will never be free from needing God. He alone is perfect, valiant, complete. And in him, so are you. But only *in him*.

Dear God, I'm sorry. Please forgive me for failing to live and love in the way you want me to. Thank you that the blood of Jesus cleanses me from all sin. Fill me afresh with your Spirit now, Lord, that I may walk in love and freedom and bring you delight and pleasure! In Jesus's name I pray.

the fight of faith

Now the Lord is the Spirit, and where the
Spirit of the Lord is, there is freedom.
—2 Corinthians 3:17

The other night I was lying on the floor with worship music playing. But I wasn't lying on the floor worshipping. I was wondering. The day had not been a great one. I was exhausted from travel and too many conversations, and I thought the answer to my physical and emotional state would be found in pizza and chocolate ice cream. I chose to spend the entire day in old patterns of living that have never proven helpful.

Lying on the floor, listening to the music, I asked God, *Do you really love me now? Here? How can you possibly love me in this low place?*

But I knew he did. Jesus died on the cross for all my sins, even the ones I have committed over and over and over again. There was a battle going on for my freedom that day. And it was raging where it almost always rages: over what I would choose to believe.

Jesus has won our freedom in a spiritual show-down with Satan. But our Enemy still refuses to go down without a fight. He knows he cannot take down Jesus, the Victorious One. But he can still wound his heart by wounding ours. Jesus has won our freedom. But we need to receive it, claim it, and stand in it. That is our good fight of faith: believing God is who he says he is and believing we are who he says we are in the face of evidence surrounding us that screams the opposite.

In order for us to live in freedom and become the women we are to become, we need to receive God's love even in our lowest places.

Jesus, I long to be free. I long to know you and love you more deeply. You are worthy. Please remove everything that separates me from knowing you as you truly are and keeps me from living in the freedom you have purchased for me. In Jesus's mighty name, amen.

agreeing with God

We demolish arguments and every pretension that sets itself up against the knowledge of God, and we take captive every thought to make it obedient to Christ.
—2 Corinthians 10:5

Descartes famously wrote, "I think, therefore I am." I would add a fill-in-the-blank in each phrase. I think I am _____, therefore I am _____. I think I am kind, therefore I am kind. I think I am chosen, therefore I am chosen. I think I am becoming more loving, therefore I am becoming more loving. I think I am forever bound to sin, therefore I am forever bound to sin.

What do you think about God? What do you think about yourself? Who are you? What do you think life is about? What do you think is true? What we think informs our reality and has a direct effect on how we live our lives. What we focus on, we move toward.

What we look at, esteem, molds us in its direction. What we think is true plays out in our moment-by-moment existence. What are you thinking?

We can no longer afford to let our thoughts run wild. What we think on *matters*. We have to make it a practice to regularly check in on our hearts, our thoughts. What are we believing? What agreements are we making? Why? When we become aware that our thoughts are not aligned with the Word of God, we repent and elevate our thoughts to agree with God. When we become aware of agreements we are making with the Enemy, like, "Life is hard, then you die," or "I will never change," we break those agreements. Out loud. Regardless of how you feel.

Break any agreement you are making that goes against the Word of God with this prayer:

I renounce this lie. I break every agreement I have been making with my Enemy. I renounce the agreement that [I am overwhelmed; I'll never get free; I hate so-and-so; I am stupid, ugly, fat, depressed—name it, and break with it]. I renounce this in the name of Jesus Christ, my Lord.

---

worthy of our yes

How will this be …?
—Luke 1:34

Mary was a young woman between thirteen and fifteen years old when the angel Gabriel appeared to her and told her she would bear the son of God.

She asked with expectancy, "How *will* God do this, since I am a virgin?" It is not a question of doubt. It is a question *rooted in faith*. Mary immediately believed Gabriel. When confronted with the miraculous, Mary asked how *will*. She knew that if God says something—anything—we can believe him.

Mary knew God before she ever carried him in her womb. Before the angel ever spoke those words, she knew that nothing is impossible for God. No matter how troubled Mary was, her heart had been cultivated by faith. In other words, *I belong to him. I am his. So yes, Lord.*

Did Mary know what this was going to mean for her? Maybe. Was she afraid? Maybe. She was a human being. She knew better than anyone else her weaknesses. And God chose her. He chose her to bring the Savior of the world to the world just as God has chosen us to bring the Savior of the world to our world. Mary believed God and knew that he was worthy of her yes.

Mary was a very young woman of very profound faith. How good it is to follow in her footsteps. To respond as she did and believe—not asking *how* God can come but simply expecting that he will.

Jesus, when you tell me what you want to do in my life, may my response be simply, "How will this be?"

81

an active imagination

Whatever is true, whatever is noble, whatever
is right, whatever is pure, whatever is lovely,
whatever is admirable—if anything is excellent
or praiseworthy—think about such things.
—Philippians 4:8

One of the next times we meet Mary is on the night of Jesus's birth. The shepherds tell her and Joseph of the angel's proclamation. How encouraging that must have been! Afterward, Scripture says, "Mary treasured up all these things and pondered them in her heart" (Luke 2:19).

Mary *actively remembered*. Late at night, while nursing her little baby, she would pull out these treasures and think on them. She was a woman of wisdom who knew what to store in her heart, what to treasure, what to ponder.

What are you pondering today? What do you ponder in the middle of the night when you can't sleep?

When all is quiet outside of you, what is going on inside of you? Many of us ponder our failures, our disappointments of the day, the week, the month, our lives. Or the failures of others who have disappointed us.

Those are not treasures. Their names are accusations, regrets, and resentments. Pondering on these will not bring life to our souls.

Treasures are true. They are what Paul encourages us to ponder: the right, the pure, the lovely, the admirable. Treasures are Scripture. Treasures include remembering what God has said and done and promised he will do. The greatest treasure of all is Jesus himself. What about lying in bed and thinking about him?

Try it tonight. Let your imagination—consecrated to Jesus—go. How handsome he is! How strong! How brave! How courageous, bold, noble, kingly, and glorious! What a great singer he is! What a great dancer! You name it, he's the best at it! And he wants you! You—yes, you—have been chosen by the King of Kings. Ponder that. Treasure it in your heart.

What image of God might you remember this week when you are feeling overwhelmed, fearful, or less than beautiful?

82

when God lingers

*Now Jesus loved Martha and her sister and Lazarus.
So, when he heard that Lazarus was ill, he stayed
two days longer in the place where he was.*
—John 11:5–6 ESV

When Jesus heard that his good friend Lazarus was dying, he didn't rush to Lazarus's side. He had something even better in mind.

So he waited where he was. And then he performed one of the greatest miracles of his earthly ministry.

Just as we have to do so often, Lazarus's sisters had to wait for God to come, realizing he wasn't going to come at the time they wanted.

Believing God is good in the midst of waiting is incredibly hard. Believing God is good in the midst of immense sorrow, loss, or pain is even more difficult. Those are the times that test our faith, transforming it to gold. What we come to know of God and the terrain he comes to inhabit in our hearts through trials leads people to say, "I wouldn't change a thing." That's the crazy, supernatural realm of God.

I know that many times God didn't answer your prayers in the way you wanted or in the timing you wanted. That was what Mary experienced when Jesus did not come and Lazarus died. Yet when Mary saw Jesus coming, she ran to him and fell at his feet. She worshipped him. She brought to Jesus the whole truth of who she was, including her profound grief and uncontrolled weeping. And in seeing her weeping, Jesus cried too.

Your tears move Jesus. Your waiting. Your love. Your sorrows. He is moved when you worship him even though it all looks hopeless. It is one of the deepest ways you can express your love for him. And one of the greatest times for him to show his love for you.

Jesus, I am waiting on you today. I have been waiting on you for a long time to come and heal certain areas of my life! And in the waiting, I worship you. I love you. I believe that you see me and will come soon to bring new life. In Jesus's name, amen.

lavish love

Then Mary took about a pint of pure nard, an expensive perfume; she poured it on Jesus' feet and wiped his feet with her hair. And the house was filled with the fragrance of the perfume.
—John 12:3

Days after Jesus rose Lazarus from the dead, he was having dinner with his friends. That's when Mary did the unthinkable. She came into the room with an alabaster jar of very expensive perfume. (Many commentators believe this perfume was her life savings.) Mary broke the neck of the jar open and slowly poured some of the perfume on Jesus's head and then poured the rest on his feet. Then she did something extremely intimate and scandalous. She unbound her hair and wiped his feet with it, even though a respectable woman did not let down her hair in public.

The fragrance of Mary's offering filled the room. There was a *change in the atmosphere*. When we pour out all we have in worship to Jesus, others around us sense the beauty of that offering.

But the Gospels tell us that those present that evening were indignant and rebuked her harshly. "What a waste of money! A whole year's wages poured out for nothing! Think of how many poor families could eat for a week on that."

Have you ever had your motives misunderstood? Have you ever had someone criticize the way you worship or spend your time or money, the way you minister or believe or come through or don't come through? Jesus knows well that it hurts to be misunderstood and judged. He knows it is part of the sorrow of living in a fallen world.

Jesus always defends a worshipper, and that night he defended Mary's reckless devotion. Jesus "got" Mary, and he "gets" you. He understood her heart and the depth of her love. She had her unique portion, true to her, and she gave it all.

Mary ministered to Jesus in a way that no one else even comprehended, because she knew him. She trusted him. She worshipped him lavishly.

And Jesus *loved* it.

Jesus, I want to worship you today with the abandon and intimacy that Mary had when she poured perfume on your feet. I want to worship you lavishly! Amen.

84

---

you are chosen

*For he chose us in him before the creation of the
world to be holy and blameless in his sight.*
—Ephesians 1:4

Growing up, I wasn't athletic. I was never picked first for
the team, and I was never once asked to a dance. When
I was in the fourth grade, however, my classmates chose
me to be Citizen of the Year. I still remember the joy
of it. Each day throughout the year, our teacher chose
one student to be Citizen of the Day. Their name went
up on the special chart for all to see. On the last day
of school, the teacher tallied up the names to see who
had won the honor most often. It turned out to be a tie
between me and a cute boy named Bobby. So she took
a private vote. There were more boys in the classroom
than girls, so I was pretty certain I wouldn't win. But I
had an edge. My family was moving in a week from our
home in Prairie Village, Kansas, to unknown California.

I was leaving, and everyone knew it. This could be my good-bye present. And I did win.

I didn't really care why I won. I simply cared that *I* was chosen. My prize was a certificate and the cardboard sheet with the school photos of all my classmates. I pulled their photos off the board, put them in an envelope, and took them with me to California.

That was the spring immediately before what would become the earthquake of my young life. When we got to our new state, my family utterly fell apart. How many times did I go to my little box, pore over my classmates' pictures, and remember that I was loved? That I had been chosen? It was a God-given lifeline of remembrance when I needed it most.

Did you know that God chooses *you*? He chooses you to be in relationship with him. He chooses you to know his peace. He chooses you to receive his salvation.

When your world shakes and crumbles, remember this truth: you are chosen. Nothing will ever change that.

Jesus, I love that you have reached for me. Not for who I wish you had made me to be or who I yearn to be someday, but just for me, now, in my messiness, in the process of you transforming me! Amen.

85

a divine exchange

Teach me your ways, O LORD,
that I may live according to your truth!
Grant me purity of heart,
so that I may honor you.
With all my heart I will praise you, O Lord my God.
I will give glory to your name forever,
for your love for me is very great.
—Psalm 86:11–13 NLT

One of the best ways to help us remember who our God is and who we are to him is to worship him. In worship, when we turn the gaze of our hearts away from ourselves and our needs and onto Jesus, a divine shift happens that brings a great good to our lives. Our enormous struggles and concerns become much less overwhelming in the face of our powerful, loving Jesus. In worship, we remember that we have been bought with his precious blood. We remember who we belong to.

You are Jesus's beloved: "I belong to my beloved, and his desire is for me" (Song of Songs 7:10). He cares for you and those you love beyond telling. You are forever loved.

Worshipping God is our response to being loved, forgiven, and known. It is our chance to offer our thanks for being seen, chosen, wanted, understood, cherished, and made new! Worship is our response to seeing Jesus as he really is: worthy, beautiful, endlessly good, kind, forgiving, generous, wonderful, and utterly and completely *for* us.

Worship is an encounter with God that changes us by aligning our spirits with truth even when it doesn't *feel* true. We pour ourselves out onto him, and he pours himself into us. It is a divine exchange that ministers to his heart and renews our own.

Intimate worship is simply telling God how wonderful he is and why. It is pouring out our love onto him like oil. We bring him all that we are as women, even our weariness and sorrow. In our loving of Jesus, we become increasingly available for him to continue his deep work in us, transforming us into the women we long to be.

Jesus, I give you my weariness. I give you my doubt. I give you my desire to give up. I come with my thirst. I offer you my desire, my gifting, my weakness, my need, my failure, my everything. I give you all that I am, God. I give you my love.

86

"she was with Jesus"

Whom have I in heaven but you?
And earth has nothing I desire besides you.
My flesh and my heart may fail,
but God is the strength of my heart
and my portion forever.
—Psalm 73:25–26

Our worship of Jesus pushes back the kingdom of darkness and ushers in the kingdom of God. It changes the atmosphere around us so that others can sense, *She was with Jesus.*

Why don't you take a few minutes and come before him now? Imagine you are sitting at his feet and listening, or washing his feet with your tears, or gazing up at him on the cross, or even bowing before the very much alive and risen Lord. There is no doing this wrong. It makes God so happy when we pause in the midst of our day or create an extended time alone with him, simply to adore him!

Jesus is worthy of our devotion and thanks. Your Jesus is the One who rode into the depths of the darkest, most dangerous dungeon to rescue his true love. He is the One who will ride again on a white steed with fire in his eyes and a flaming sword in his hand. He has inscribed you into the palm of his nail-pierced hand. He knows your every thought, numbers your every hair, and cherishes your every tear. Jesus weeps for you and with you, longs for you, hopes for you, dreams of you, and rejoices over you with singing. He is the One who has battled all the forces of hell to free you and who battles still.

Jesus is your knight in shining armor. He is the love you have been longing for. He is your dream come true. He is your hero. He is Aslan, the Lion of Judah, and the Lamb of God. He is the Prince of Peace, the Alpha and Omega, the First and the Last, the King of Kings and the Lord of Lords, the Mighty One.

His name is like a kiss and an earthquake. His gaze is on you. He has pledged his love to you and betrothed you to himself forever. He is unchangeable, and his love will never fail you.

How will you respond? Love him. Adore him. Worship him.

God, whom do I have in heaven but you? And earth has nothing I desire besides you. My flesh and my heart may fail, but you are the strength of my heart and my portion forever.

87

---

your true name

You will be called by a new name
that the mouth of the LORD will bestow.
—Isaiah 62:2

As women growing in our own becoming, we want to live with holy intention. We want to be awake to the present moment, those around us, the Spirit within us, and our own souls. We are meant to live lives of significance. It is right that we desire to live for a purpose higher than protecting our skin from sun damage and being well liked. We want to live unto a high calling and a meaningful purpose, and that purpose flows out of our identity.

Knowing who we are enables us to live the life we have been born to live—the life the seen and unseen world needs us to live. We need to know who we are and own who we are. Who *are* you? What is your identity—*really*?

You are a new creation in Christ, more than a conqueror. Victorious. Strong. Empowered. Safe. Secure. Sealed. You are a channel of the life and love of God. You are alive in Christ. You are the beloved of God. You are his.

Who is Jesus? He is the love you have been looking for all your life, and he has never taken his eyes off of you. He has a name for you that he wants you to fully become; he holds your true identity, and this is what you are meant to grow into. So you'll want to ask Jesus your true name (or names—he often has several for us). As he tells you, dear one, choose to believe.

Jesus, I choose to believe that I am your beloved and that your desire is for me. I choose to believe that I am no longer forsaken or deserted but that I am your delight, sought after and dearly loved. Jesus, I want to become the woman you have in mind for me to be. Show me who she is; show me who I really am, who I was always meant to be. Tell me my true name; give me an image of who you see me becoming. Give me eyes to see and ears to hear and the courage to accept what you are saying. Tell me, Jesus.

---

what the world needs now

Seek ye first the kingdom of God, and his righteousness;
and all these things shall be added unto you.
—Matthew 6:33 KJV

We will never be happy as long as we are trying to live apart from ourselves or in disregard of ourselves, our hearts, our desires, our ache. Though happiness is never the highest goal, it comes to us naturally when the other aspects of our lives are in order.

Love is always the highest goal. Love of God, of others, and of ourselves, of the woman God has created us to be. We don't want to live in spite of ourselves, but we want to embrace ourselves, owning the multifaceted mysterious women we are and the unique way we bring Jesus to the world.

You are the only you there has ever been or ever will be.

God made you *you* on purpose. Now. For a reason.

The world does not need yet another woman who despises the lovely creation that she is. God does not long for another woman who rejects herself and, by extension, him. The world needs a woman who is thankful for how God has made her, who trusts that he is transforming her, and who actually enjoys who she is. It's a good thing to like who you are. God likes you! We get to like ourselves too. When you like yourself, you are free to enjoy others, and in your presence people experience an invitation to become and enjoy who they truly are as well.

Jesus, you are transforming me into your image. What part do you want me to play in that transformation today? Show me how you want me to see you. Show me how you want me to see myself! In Jesus's name, amen.

who do you think you are?

I have loved you with an everlasting love; I
have drawn you with unfailing kindness.
—Jeremiah 31:3

About twenty years ago, I was at church and in a very low place. I felt hideously ugly. I was telling myself that I looked like Jabba the Hutt. (Not very nice words to say to oneself—remember the power of naming things.) Kneeling in prayer, I asked God, *How do you see me?* In my sanctified imagination, I immediately saw a woman kneeling. The sun filtering through the window framed her in a golden beam of light. She was wearing a lovely fitted white satin dress. Her hair was softly yet ornately done up with seed pearls in it. She was beautiful, a bride clearly held in the gaze of her God.

He saw me then as beautiful. He sees me now as beautiful.

When God looks at his daughter—me, you, any beloved one—he does not view her through the veil of her sin, the shroud of her failures, or the canopy of her past. When God looks at us, he sees us through the blood of Jesus. When God looks at you, he sees a masterpiece. He sees his beloved bride. We must remember to view ourselves as he does! Both who we are in this moment and the woman he is forming in us.

Who do you think you are? Who are you on the road to becoming? Do you have a vision of who you could become? How does God see you? What is his vision of who you are to become? It's vital that we ask him that question. And then wait for his answer.

Having a vision of who you are becoming informs your present. We live today knowing who we are going to be tomorrow. The key is to *choose to believe* we are who God says we are. And then rest in the knowledge that God is the one responsible for our transformation. We lean into him. We will fail. He will not.

How do you see me, God? Please give me your vision of the woman I am to become.

Write down what you hear from God or merely
what, by faith, you choose to believe is becoming
true for you because you want it.

90

---

you are the beloved

I am my beloved's, and my beloved is mine.
—Song of Solomon 6:3 KJV

What we think, we become.

In the midst of your day—in the mess, the mundane, the glorious—when you laugh and live well and when you don't, get into the habit of stopping and asking yourself, *What am I thinking is true about myself?* If it does not line up with the Word of God, reject it as a lie. Replace it with the truth.

What would it be like right now to entertain the possibility in your heart that all God says about you is true?

You are his delight.

You make him happy just by being you.

He thinks you're lovely.

You are his beloved.

You are the one who has captured his heart.

What difference would it make in your life if these things really were true? Think of it. Let your heart go there for a moment. Because it does make all the difference in the world.

Ask God, *Am I your beloved? How do you see me? Do you delight in me? Do you love me because you're God and that's your job, or do you love me simply for me?*

You, dear heart, you *are* the beloved.

Jesus, thank you for this truth about me. I receive it. I agree with you, and I declare that I am your daughter. I am chosen, holy, and dearly loved. I am the apple of your eye. I am your beloved, and your desire is for me. Please write this truth deep in my heart. In Jesus's name I pray. Amen.

a few final words from stasi

Dear one, you are beautiful, and your beauty is increasing. It's growing! You are becoming more and more the lovely, courageous woman of God he created you to be.

The more we know Jesus as he really is, the more we love him. The more we love him, the more our lives are transformed. God is the One who gives us the confidence to become. Who gives us the vision to see ourselves as he sees us. Who gives us the courage and wisdom to believe that what he says about us is true.

My sister, you will not be able to do it perfectly. But Jesus has and will. Because of Jesus, you can fight well. Pray well. Listen well. Live well. Serve well. Love well. Become well. One day, Christ will tell you your story, and you will be amazed at the glory, the beauty, the redemption, and the presence of Jesus throughout your life in ways you can't even now imagine. Because you are beautiful. Now.

God is a
dreamer.
He has dreams of you.
And for you.

—stasi eldredge, becoming myself

This powerful series will take you deeper into your own story as you become the woman God desires you to be. Stasi ushers women into an authentic journey of freedom, healing, and transformation. Explore God's intimate involvement in your past and his unique dreams for your future.